SANDY KOUFAX

Strikeout King

When the Dodgers humbled the New York Yankees by taking the 1963 World Series, four games to none, it was Sanford "Sandy" Koufax who won the first and fourth games. Sandy is a pitcher whose accomplishments include two 18-strikeout performances and two no-hitters, in addition to his championship performances in the 1963 Series. Yet, Koufax is a team player, and gets his thrills not from recognition as a top performer, but as a member of the most successful National League team in recent major league history.

SANDY KOUFAX

Strikeout King

By Arnold Hano

G. P. Putnam's Sons

New York

Fifth Impression

Published simultaneously in the Dominion of
Canada by Longmans Canada Limited, Toronto
Library of Congress Catalog Card Number: 64-19920
MANUFACTURED IN THE UNITED STATES OF AMERICA

To Laurie and Steve

CONTENTS

SANDY KOUFAX

Strikeout King

1

The Word Is Dominates

"LOS ANGELES is the city of the blind," the late novelist Nathanael West once wrote, and on the evening of June 30, 1962, the label was never more apt. At least, that's how the New York Mets must have felt.

On that night, at Dodger Stadium, nestled in a ravine in Elysian Park in Los Angeles, a young man with a ropelike left arm threw baseballs so swiftly through the darkness that all you could see was a thin pale blur. The young man was Sanford (Sandy) Koufax, twenty-six and a half years old to the day, and the men who searched the darkness for the ball that evening were the New York Mets. They searched in vain. Sandy Koufax threw a no-hitter.

When you speak about Sandy Koufax, you have to count his no-hitters, just as you had to count Bob Feller's. This was Koufax's first. The next year he threw another. Does anyone among us wish to risk the opinion Sandy Koufax will never throw another?

I went to the game that night. It was, on the face of it, a gross mismatch. Sandy Koufax, and the Dodgers, versus the New York Mets. The finest pitcher in baseball against the weakest-hitting team in baseball.

And so you must not consider me a prophet when I said to nobody in particular after the first inning of the game: "He's going to pitch a no-hitter."

Why not? In the first inning, Sandy Koufax pitched perfectly. Literally, perfectly. Nine times he threw the baseball. Nine strikes. Not a foul tip in the lot. Three outs. Three strikeouts. A man in front of me looked back after I had made my prediction, and said: "Heck, he's going to strike out twenty-seven men."

That is how overpowering Sandy Koufax appeared. He did not strike out twenty-seven men. Only thirteen. There wasn't a base hit in the Met lineup. With two minor exceptions, there wasn't a near hit. In the second inning, after Koufax had struck out Richie Ashburn, Rod Kanehl, and Felix Mantilla on nine pitches, Frank Thomas hit a ground ball into the hole between short and third. Maury Wills rushed over, fielded the ground ball, and fired to Ron Fairly at first. Frank Thomas does not run well these days, or those days either, and the play at first was not close. Still, Wills had gone a long way, and had made a long throw, and the play remains the defensive standout of the evening. In the sixth inning, after Koufax had again struck out three men in a row—Elio Chacon, to close out the fifth, Chris Cannizzaro and pitcher Ray Daviault—Ashburn hit a curling line drive into left center field. Left fielder Tommy Davis broke quickly for the ball, seemed to hesitate, and then caught the drive somewhat in the manner of a farmer surrounding a pig on the loose. It turned out that Davis had

momentarily lost the ball in the arc lights. But he recovered nicely, and the no-hitter was secure.

Pitching no-hitters is every pitcher's business. You begin every game with a no-hitter. Eventually there comes that first hit, and you go on from there, hoping to throw a one-hitter. Usually you end up in a warm shower, around the sixth or seventh inning, dreaming of the next start, which will begin with a no-hitter. Until.

You go to ball games in the hope of seeing the unusual. A bases-loaded home run. A triple play. A piece of daring baserunning. A startling bare-handed stop of a ground ball that results in a force-out at second. An umpire calling one correctly. Or that gorgeous rarity, a no-hitter. You go, and as the innings creep by and the outs pile up, you become victim of a mounting and exquisite tension that has few equals in sports. It is the boy with his finger in the dike, thwarting the sea. It is Atlas, struggling to hold aloft the world. Will the sea break through? Will the earth topple?

The pressure is so real it becomes nearly visible. And when the no-hitter is completed, you explode with sheer relief; you are buoyant at release from a confining agony.

That is, if the pitcher is anybody today but Sandy Koufax. Koufax has come to dominate pitching as has nobody since Bob Feller or Dizzy Dean. This is not to say there are no other great pitchers. There are, and many. Juan Marichal—who also pitched a no-hitter in 1963—is a joy to watch, a big-stepping, high-kicking youngster who throws baseballs with fierce glee, and who seems to enjoy

himself as much as any man in the game these days. Jim Maloney, a big blond young man with a serious face and a solemn manner, hurls baseballs with terrifying speed. Warren Spahn, that wise old owl. Whitey Ford, Gary Peters, Camilo Pascual. Koufax's own teammate, Don Drysdale, a side-winding young man who steps to his right, uncoils his long right arm and bullets baseballs past quaking batters. And many more.

But the word is *dominates*. I do not pretend to be a baseball seer. I am an observer, and have been an observer of major-league baseball for nearly forty years now. I cannot tell you of Christy Mathewson—whose strikeout record Sandy Koufax has broken—because I never saw Mathewson. I cannot tell you of Walter Johnson, because if I ever saw Johnson, I do not remember. I never saw Rube Waddell who, some say, threw his left-handed pitches even more swiftly than does Koufax.

But I saw Dazzy Vance. I saw Hubbell and Dean and Feller. Newhouser and Grove and Pete Alexander. I sat in the right field seats—as a fan; not as a reporter, but simply an observer—the day Don Larsen threw his perfect no-hitter against the Dodgers. Nor do you need a no-hitter to dominate a game.

I remember a game pitched by Clay Bryant, against the New York Giants, when Bryant was a young rawboned youngster with the Chicago Cubs. Later, Bryant hurt his arm and lost his effectiveness, but on this afternoon years ago Clay Bryant was as overpowering a pitcher as I can

recall for a nine-inning stretch. He shut out the Giants on two hits that day, and the Giant hitters looked helpless before the flaming fast balls Bryant poured through.

I remember a World Series game in 1936, pitched by Monte Pearson, a man whose reputation is that of a curve-ball pitcher. On that Sunday afternoon, pitching against Carl Hubbell and the Giants, Pearson was as fast as a man can be, whistling his pitches past such Giant hitters as Mel Ott, Bill Terry, and Travis Jackson.

And I remember a Memorial Day doubleheader back in the mid-Thirties, Roy Parmalee, whom we called Tarzan, throwing his deceptive swift stuff against the Brooklyn Dodgers. Big Parmalee had an easy overhand motion, a man who looked as though he were playing catch, but the ball suddenly came out of that motion, a tiny pellet delivered with tremendous speed. The Dodgers appeared futile that day as Parmalee shut them out on two dinky hits.

These pitchers dominated a game on the days I have described. But Koufax matches them, day after day. With the exception of Bob Feller and the occasional exception of Dizzy Dean, I have never seen a pitcher who so completely dominates any game as does Sandy Koufax. Koufax, on the mound, is an absolute master. They tell me some pitchers today throw as swiftly as or perhaps even more swiftly than Koufax. Some curves explode more sharply. Some change-ups are more baffling. There are ways of measuring these things—speed meters and photographs and the like. I must shrug my shoulders and rely on the naked eye, searching for

that pale blur. "Either he throws the fastest ball I've ever batted against, or else I'm going blind," is the way Richie Ashburn put it after the June 30, 1962 no-hit, no-run game. Either Koufax throws the most completely unhittable pitches, or else I am going blind.

Bob Feller had this talent. He reared back and fired his fast balls, and all you saw was a long, lean curl of light whisking past the flailing bat. If Koufax achieved a perfect inning when he used nine pitches to strike out three Mets to open his no-hitter, then I recall seeing Bob Feller pitch perfectly to two men in the 1939 All-Star game, at Yankee Stadium. The two men were Johnny Mize and Dolph Camilli, and neither Mize nor Camilli bears any resemblance to the hitters in the New York Met lineup. Feller threw his fast ball six times to Mize and Camilli, and the big left-handed sluggers took their toehold and swung. Six strikes. Not a foul. Perfect pitching by a man who everybody expected to throw fast balls, and who did throw fast balls right on by two of the best hitters in the league. But what fast balls!

Once in a while you see another man with this overpowering speed. Perhaps the speed meters will say that Steve Barber is faster (as a meter once did say) or that teammate Don Drysdale is faster, or that St. Louis Cardinal pitcher Bob Gibson is faster. Ask the man who knows. Ask the hitter. The hitters will tell you. Koufax is the answer. Koufax—today—is baseball's supreme pitcher, a man who can unloose a baseball inning after inning that jets past a

hitter before he can truly uncoil. When Koufax throws, you just do not expect a hitter to hit. It is as simple, and as awesome, as that. Other pitchers may pitch no-hitters. It is a surprise when Sandy Koufax doesn't.

You must forgive this introduction. I enjoy baseball. I marvel at the skill you see on the diamond. I am struck by the ballet-like beauty of the double play. I relish the craft of the well-executed hit-and-run. I am charged up by the line drive that is driven between two outfielders, and the race that ensues between a thrown ball and a running man as he digs for third base.

But the game is pitching. There is a quality to pitching that is nearly as elemental as the brutelike symbol of a man lugging his bat to the plate in the fashion of cavemen carrying their clubs to combat. Pitching is a refined symbol of other, elemental combat. When man wanted to dispose of his foe—whether he was another man or a shaggy four-footed beast of the fields—he learned to shatter his foe's skull with a thrown rock. Later, it was an arrow he contrived to throw through the air at his feared target. All this is some form of pitching, if I may put the cart before the horse.

Pitching—of stones, of arrows, of bullets—was man's first sophisticated weapon. When David did battle with Goliath, he knew enough to stay his distance, but he also knew how to bring down his foe, pitching his slingshot rock against Goliath's brow. Men have thrown with speed and accuracy and destructive effect through the centuries of

time. Today's pitcher was yesterday's spear thrower. Today's pitcher was yesterday's Captain Ahab, hurling his harpoon into the side of the white whale. The Greeks cherished various forms of pitching—men throwing the discus, the javelin, the heavy shot put. Men in battle have rushed to the very mouth of huge cannon and thick defense works, and with a weapon no bigger than a tennis ball, they have thrown this weapon—a hand grenade—against the defense works and at the cannon, and destroyed both. Jove threw thunderbolts.

Nor is throwing reserved only for destruction. The classic form of slapstick humor is a pie, thrown in a man's face. There is something about throwing that delights us. It disarms the bigger man, it overthrows pomp, it is the weapon of the underdog, the weapon of an emerging intelligence.

And in baseball, pitching dominates. Even in this era of home-run hitting, pitching dominates. Pitchers, with their extraordinary skill, have learned to thwart these latter-day cavemen, these Goliaths who could crush a man's cranium with their bare hands were they fortunate enough to get in close. The pitcher keeps them away. The game is pitching.

Nothing can occur in a ball game until the pitcher throws the ball. He is the lord of the park. The game begins at his signal. And what goes on on the mound determines the outcome of the game. Even the fact that there is a mound is but another subtle indication of the lordly characteristic of the pitcher. They build a small hill for the pitcher, and he mounts the hill as a king mounts his throne. There is actu-

ally no real need for a pitcher's mound. Pitchers themselves admit it does little if any good. But it serves to remind us who is the true master of the game.

And they are the masters. The finest hitters in baseball—the Cobbs and Ruths and Hornsbys and Williamses and Musials—will make out more often than they will hit safely. Of all the lords of pitching today, Sandy Koufax is the most lordly. As such, he dominates the sport. Nor is it simply my own prejudiced opinion. The Los Angeles Dodgers employ a gentleman named Allan Roth to keep the team's statistics. Statistician Roth sees and charts every pitch Sandy Koufax makes. Recently Roth said of Sandy Koufax:

"It's reached the point now where when anybody gets a hit off him, people turn to each other and say, 'Gee, I wonder what he did wrong?' "

But—you say—that's the company man speaking up. Let's hear from the "enemy."

Gene Mauch, the personable and intelligent manager of the Philadelphia Phillies, says:

"If Koufax starts thirty-five games, you won't be surprised if he wins thirty-five. It's news when he loses."

Eighty-year-old Frank Shaugnessy—one-time commissioner of minor-league ball, and a man who has watched all the great pitchers of this century—says Koufax is the "most unhittable" he has ever seen.

Said Yogi Berra, after the first World Series game of 1963: "I don't see how he lost five games during the season."

Willie Mays: "He's got a fast ball that, man, you just can't see."

Gene Woodling: "Sandy is the kind of guy who sends you back to the farm—and happy to go."

These men are saying the same thing. It astounds Mauch and Berra when Koufax loses. Mays has trouble seeing the fast ball. Shaugnessy is surprised when a batter gets his bat in front of a Koufax pitch. Unhittable, unseeable, unlosable. And the batter knows it.

This notion of Koufax's unhittableness was once put to the test. An erudite college-baseball coach evolved a rather esoteric theory that declared, in substance, that a strong, healthy, sharp-eyed young man with a baseball bat would always be able to hit a thrown baseball provided he followed certain rules of behavior at the plate. Stance, swing, and the rest. The coach, together with his brawny, equally erudite pupil, appeared on an Art Linkletter television show one evening to put the theory into practice. Pitted against this display of brainpower and mathematical certainties was Sandy Koufax.

Koufax threw four pitches to the college youth. He threw four times, because—eureka!—the batter ticked one pitch foul. The other three times the batter connected solidly and satisfyingly with a rush of wind whipped up by Koufax's fast ball.

So much for one theory. On the other side of the fence, and obviously stationed with the oddsmakers, a California physicist, Dr. Paul Kilpatrick, in September of 1963, came

up with another theory. This one stated that there are twenty-six ways for a batter to miss a pitched ball. Twenty-six factors that intrude themselves when a batter swings. The good physicist measured these factors—the bat's tilt, the angle of the swing, the speed of the swing, the timing mechanism that sends nerve waves from eye to brain to wrists and legs, and a whole caboodle of other ingredients. He actually plotted an equation full of x's and y's and square roots and other exotic plants that explained it all and ran the width of a page and then some.

When the doctor was finished, he had satisfactorily proved on paper what the rest of us already knew. We had seen Sandy Koufax. Coincidentally, the day Dr. Kilpatrick's theory was released to the waiting world, Sandy Koufax pitched his eleventh shutout of the season, to break the record for National League left-handers.

Still—and despite the introduction—this is no Superman. And were it a Superman, it would be deadly dull, either to watch or to read about.

Sandy Koufax is more than just a baseball pitcher. He is the center of an adoring public. Fifty people write to him every day, fan letters, and many of these are from lady fans with romance in their heart. Sandy Koufax earns well over $60,000 in salary, and many other thousands of dollars in testimonials, television appearances, night-club appearances, and the like. He has mastered his trade, and can look out on a benevolent and warm world. Happiness is a no-hitter, a pennant, a World Series victory. Happiness is a

strikeout record. Happiness is money, good looks; happiness is a crowd's ovation.

But Sandy Koufax is a human being. He says, with a patience that must wear thin: "What people have to understand is that maybe I threw just about the right pitch. But that's a major-league batter up there at the plate with a bat in his hands, and maybe *he* did something right."

Twenty-six ways to miss a ball, and sometimes they all fail, and a baseball soars out of sight. Sandy Koufax is a human being with human frailties. Some of them have been physical, and terrifying. The finest pitcher in baseball was—a year earlier—a man who nearly had his left index finger amputated. He has suffered shoulder aches, sprained ankles, a tumor on his ribs, an ulcerated toe, many other ills. He is a young man once so discouraged by his progress, or lack of, he came close to quitting the sport he now dominates. He was a man who fought with his general manager, right out on the ball field, begging for a chance to pitch and prove himself. And he is a man who—even during the superb year he enjoyed in 1963—could say to magazine writer Jack Olsen:

"There are other things to think about. Sometimes it seems like a dream world. It seems I should have everything a man could want now, but who knows what's going to happen? When is it going to end? I feel that if I could play till I'm forty or thirty-eight or thirty-six and be successful till then, sure, then I would have everything I want. But if it's over next year, what have I got? The money I've made I

could spend in a very short time. I have some schooling but I'm not really prepared to do anything but pitch. The thought is always there that it might end quickly. I remember too many great arms, too many pitchers that everybody thought were going to be great, and all of a sudden, it was over."

This, too, is Sandy Koufax. A handsome, talented young man, six-feet two inches tall and 200-plus pounds, with a strong left arm and a marvelous arsenal at his command, yet a man with the thoughts and fears of any of us.

"I'll tell you," Sandy Koufax said to Jack Olsen, "some nights out there you feel alone, scared and naked."

2

K Is for Strikeout; K Is for Koufax

WITH THE EXCEPTION of bathing beauty contestants and stock market quotations, no institution in America is so closely measured as is baseball. If Willie Mays hits a home run, we are instantly told (or we will insistently demand to know) that the home run was Mays's twenty-fourth of the season, his 430th of his career, traveled over the left center field fence at the 372-foot mark, landed in the fifth row of seats (where it was caught by an eleven-year-old boy) and was the third he had hit with his new 35-inch, 32-ounce bat (originally modeled for Ted Williams). The boy's name was Larry Johnson.

Base hits are measured for length. A baseball's velocity upon leaving a pitcher's hand is solemnly clocked. The number of times a man races from first to second before the catcher's throw gets to the second baseman or the shortstop is duly acknowledged. Wins, losses, runs batted in, balks. Singles, doubles, triples, homers. Double plays, and double plays grounded into by right-handed batters. The distance in feet Al Dark throws a stool in a clubhouse.

We baseball fans are apparently fascinated by these numbers. They rattle about our heads. The fact is, the numbers have some virtue. If a man hits forty home runs, he is obviously a greater home-run hitter than a man who hits four home runs. So it goes with pitching. The twenty-game winner is probably a far finer pitcher than the twenty-game loser, although not necessarily.

Still, there must be a disclaimer before any citing of statistics. Baseball figures often distort. What is probably worse, baseball figurers, such as myself, pick and choose our figures with loving care. When I tell you that Sandy Koufax struck out 41 men in three consecutive games in late August and early September of 1959, I will not reveal—unless pushed—that he did not win all three of the games. Just two out of three. If I chortle here in print over Koufax's 25 wins of 1963, you must remind me that Juan Marichal also won 25 in 1963, and pitched more innings. When I write that Koufax's earned-run average in 1963 was the first to dip under two runs per game in a score of years, you may cite the record of Grover Alexander who pitched five consecutive full seasons in which his *highest* ERA was 1.91.

But what is most important about numbers—baseball numbers—is to keep them in a historical perspective. Actually it is *not* obvious that the man who hits forty home runs is a greater home-run hitter than the man who hits four. When did he hit them? What pitchers did he face? Was it the era of the lively ball? John Franklin Baker used to hit eight and nine home runs in a season, for which he was

called Home Run Baker. But in hitting his eight and nine home runs against the spitter, the emery, and the shine ball of pre-World War I days, Baker may have been as great a home-run slugger as Roger Maris. Although the rules of the game have changed little through the twentieth century, the game has changed greatly. Baseball today has become a swing-from-the-heels, all-or-nothing affair, as two sets of statistics continue to demonstrate. Men hit many more home runs than ever before, batters strike out more than ever before. It is the game of the big swish, the big punch—or the big K. K is baseball's letter for strikeout, the symbol you put down on your scorecard after a hitter has fanned, and you put it down more and more these days. The game of the dead ball, of bloop hits, of pitchers who settle back and permit opposing hitters to hit the ball, secure in the knowledge that the batted ball will be confined within the spacious fences of the stadium—this game of hit-and-run, sacrifice, double-steal, and one-run-at-a-time has been largely superseded by the big swing, the big inning, the attempt to put one out of the park. Those parks are fields whose dimensions have been tampered with, to suit broad-backed sluggers. As men dig in and desperately swing longer, lighter, more whiplike bats, pitchers are more and more relying on their ability to thwart the swing entirely. A pitcher who settles back today and permits the opposition to hit away, relying on his defense, will soon test the shower-room plumbing of minor-league clubhouses.

In 1946, Detroit Tiger pitchers set a big-league one-

season record with 846 strikeouts. The record stood until a few years ago when the Dodgers became the first team to strike out more than a thousand opposing hitters. Now the Dodgers regularly strike out 1,000 men every year. In its first year in the league, the Houston Colt staff struck out over 1,000 men. In 1963, every team in the National League—with the exception of the Mets—exceeded the old Tiger mark of 846.

Home runs increase. Strikeouts increase. Batting averages dip. It's all or nothing. And so it is against a historical background of the sport that Sandy Koufax's feats must be measured. He is a strikeout pitcher, in a strikeout age.

But nothing can diminish the fact that he is the best strikeout pitcher in a strikeout age. K is for strikeout. It also must stand for Koufax. Perhaps it is more useful to think of Koufax as currently the finest strikeout artist than to compare him with Walter Johnson, or even the more modern Bob Feller.

In 1963, Sandy Koufax struck out ten or more men in a ball game on eleven separate occasions. It marked the fifty-first time Koufax had struck out ten or more men in a single game. There are pitchers today—good pitchers, winning pitchers—who will never strike out ten or more men in a single game in their entire career.

On August 31, 1959, Koufax struck out 18 San Francisco Giants in a pressure-packed ball game played before 82,000. In a strikeout age, no National Leaguer has equaled this feat. Koufax again struck out 18 men on April 24,

1962. Astonishingly, he had to repeat the trick to still cries of derision that attended the first performance. The August, 1959 game had been played at the Los Angeles Coliseum, at night, where people suggested out loud that only the poor night lights at the freakish stadium made it possible. Koufax's second 18-strikeout game occurred at Wrigley Field, Chicago, where all games are played by day. I suppose someone will now pop up with an armful of almanacs to prove the sun was in its springtime descendancy that afternoon, the visibility obscured by a smog belt cleverly imported from Los Angeles just for the occasion.

Koufax holds all sorts of other strikeout records. Only two National League pitchers have ever struck out 200 or more men in each of three consecutive seasons. Christy Mathewson is one. Sandy Koufax is the other. And Mathewson's total in his 1903, 1904, 1905 seasons is 685 strikeouts. Koufax's, for 1961, 1962, 1963, is 791.

Koufax's 15 strikeouts of the New York Yankees—daytime, again—in the first game of the 1963 World Series is a Series record. He tied a record by striking out the first five Yankees that day. His 23 strikeouts in two games of the Series is another record. Koufax's 306 strikeouts in 1963 make him the first National League pitcher of this century to whiff 300 or more men in one season. In 1961, Koufax struck out 269 men, to break Christy Mathewson's one-season league record, set 58 years ago. In 1955, in his second major-league start, nineteen-year-old Sandy Koufax —with not a single inning of minor-league experience be-

hind him—struck out 14 Cincinnati batters. No league pitcher struck out as many men in a single game all that year.

Sandy Koufax is the only starting pitcher in baseball history to average more than one strikeout per inning over his career—1,474 K's in 1,443 innings, through 1963. If you insist that many of these strikeouts came against second-division teams—as they would have to—Koufax has also struck out more than a man an inning in World Series competition, 30 strikeouts in 27 innings.

So it goes.

But if we stick with strikeouts—and the tendency is strong when you deal with a Koufax—the picture is distorted. Koufax is not simply a strikeout artist. He is a complete pitcher. Too often your strikeout king is a brute of a man who throws bullets in every direction and who bullies the hitters into meek submission. Against these wild-armed flamethrowers, batters take a gingerly stance, ready to bail out at the first opportunity. In short, men whose very effectiveness hinges on their lack of control. Sure, they strike out oodles of hitters. They also walk oodles. They wild pitch. They hit batters. They bounce pitches in front of broken-knuckled catchers. They hit the screen behind the plate, on the fly. To call them pitchers is to credit them unduly. Throwers. Not pitchers.

Sandy Koufax is a pitcher. In seven of his complete-game victories in 1963, Koufax did not walk a single man. He is not the finest control pitcher in all of baseball, but he is a

man whose control each year becomes a sharper, more delicate and accurate instrument. He can, today, pick up the corners, brush the knees, clip the shoulders. He can break off a curve that hitters "fish" for and which ends up in the dirt. Or else he'll break off another curve that batters will watch in masochistic fascination as the ball starts out too high or too wide or both, and ends up nipping a corner for a called strike.

Don Zimmer says of Koufax: "His curve is the finest I have ever seen thrown by a left-hander." It is the curve you saw on the television screen, thrown with two strikes to Tom Tresh and then to Mickey Mantle, in Koufax's second 1963 World Series effort. You remember those curves. Coming in high and wide, the batters relaxing, taking them, and then suddenly darting like a hummingbird for called third strikes. They were perfect strikes.

But not just a big curve. Koufax is mastering a change-up. In 1963, Koufax began to work on a slider. He throws all these pitches—these breaking pitches—in varying speeds.

So in Koufax you have an extraordinary fusion of blinding speed, deadly accuracy, jagged curves, and a baffling change of pace. Naturally all these contribute to the strikeout total. But far more important, they give Sandy Koufax the necessary arsenal to face any batter. He's a fast-ball hitter? Whip him up a recipe of curves, fast and slow, change-ups, slider, and the occasional Big Bertha to keep him honest. A talented curve-ball hitter, of which there are

very, very few? Waste the curve, and slip by the swift pitches. A man with undeniable power who blasts the high hard one? Slow him down, work around the knees, pitch away from his power. Koufax can do it all.

In 1963, he did do it all. Nobody won more games. His won-lost percentage, based on his 25-and-5 record, was second high in the league to teammate Ron Perranoski's 16-and-3, all in relief. His 1.88 earned-run average led both leagues by a wide margin. Only Marichal, with 321 innings, and Don Drysdale, with 315, edged Koufax's 311-inning load. His hits-per-game average was the lowest in the league. His strikeout total bested Jim Maloney, of the Reds, by 41 Ks. His eleven shutouts not only led the league but set a league record for left-handers, exceeding Carl Hubbell's ten whitewashings, established back in 1936, when Sandy Koufax was not yet a year old.

Recognition followed performance. In 1963, Sandy Koufax won enough awards, plaques, and trophies to gild every lily in Elysian Park. As the final out in the 1963 Series was being recorded, Al Silverman, editor of *Sport* magazine, announced to the press box occupants at Dodger Stadium that Koufax was the winner of a white Chevrolet Corvette, awarded each year to the Series' finest performer. Koufax, a realist, turned it in for a metal-gray job.

In quick succession, Koufax was voted National League pitcher of the year, and Comeback Man of the Year by a poll of UPI baseball writers. On October 24, he was unanimously voted the Cy Young Memorial Award, as base-

ball's outstanding pitcher. Six days later he became the National League's Most Valuable Player, the first pitcher to win the MVP since Don Newcombe, back in 1956.

He made this all-star team and that. *Sporting News* voted him player of the year. *Sport* magazine, in addition to the Corvette, selected him for the magazine's 17th annual award as "Man of the Year." Man, of course, means athlete. He was feted at 30 banquets. He topped it all off with the $10,000 Hickok belt, emblematic of professional sport's finest performer.

In the midst of these tributes, a note of moderation must be entered. The records indicate Koufax's superiority over his fellow pitchers in the year 1963. But one no-hitter does not make a career, as Bobo Holloman and Bobo Belinsky surely know. One fine summer does not dispel the past or define the future. Sandy Koufax has pitched two no-hitters? Johnny VanderMeer pitched two in a row. Koufax has now put back to back three superlative seasons? Before that, he put back-to-back six indifferent campaigns in which he lost more games than he won. Koufax owns just about every Dodger strikeout record? He also possesses the club's wild-pitch record, with 17 in 1958. Koufax is the complete pitcher? In his first eight seasons, he started and finished exactly one ball game in which he did not walk a single hitter. Once, in eight years. He blew down the Yankees in his two World Series games of 1963? With only slight quibbling, it can be pointed out that he yielded a home run in each contest, he wobbled badly in the middle innings of

the first game, and he won the second game only when Joe Pepitone lost a thrown ball against the glare of a shirt-sleeved crowd.

Perhaps we can say the same thing more kindly. When honored at a fund-raising dinner in Los Angeles in the winter of 1963–64, Koufax said joshingly: "We held the Yankees to four runs in the four-game Series. And I gave up three of them."

It is far too early to elevate Sandy Koufax to some sort of all-time pitching pedestal. Through those first nine seasons, ending in 1963, Koufax won fewer than a hundred games. Even if he puts together 25 victories a year for the next ten years—which will find him thirty-eight years old—he would still have won fewer games than Warren Spahn. As a matter of cruel fact, in 1963—Koufax's greatest season by far—the forty-three-year-old Spahn pitched two more complete games than did Sandy.

Yet figures lie. The question is not for baseball's all time. The question is now. And now—the 1963 World Series behind him—Sandy Koufax is the most dominant figure in the sport.

The comparisons you seek help make the point. Only Feller and Cy Young have thrown more no-hitters. Only Feller and Rube Waddell and Johnson have struck out more men in one season. Nobody in the National League—not Mathewson, Alexander, Vance, or any—has ever struck out as many in one year. Nobody has pitched more shutout games in one year in the past 47 years.

And always, beyond the figures, was the sense of his superiority. Warren Spahn put it best. "The Dodgers had no losing streak in 1963. Even if they lost three in a row, you knew Koufax would win the fourth." When Koufax pitched, you expected him to win. He was the stopper. He was the first man in the game to win 20 games in 1963, the first to win 25. In the month of September, when the Cardinals made their charge at the Dodgers and the Dodgers had to live down an ancient indictment of folding in the stretch, Koufax pitched and won five ball games, lost none. And he shut out the Cardinals in the second game of the desperate last-chance series back in St. Louis in the middle of the month.

It was a great year, a marvelous year, and with any luck at all, it could have been one of the finest seasons any pitcher has had in our time. There was a 1–0 loss to Cincinnati, in which Koufax yielded but three hits and struck out ten in a seven-inning stint. He lost that one. On six other occasions, he pitched well enough to win, but was not involved in any decision—a two-hitter, in six and two-third innings; a seven-hit 11-strikeout extra-inning job; a nine-hit, 10-strikeout twelve-inning performance; and a four-hitter, a five-hitter, and an eight-hitter in stints of seven or more innings. With luck and a few base hits, he would have won all of these, and the superb 1963 record would have stood at 32-and-4.

Not that Sandy Koufax needs any typewriter luck. The observer remembers Koufax's second no-hitter, thrown this

time against the Giants, who also are in no way related to the Mets. I have said earlier that Sandy Koufax is a complete pitcher. He is. But he is not a complete ballplayer, even as pitchers go. He does not field his position terribly well. He has trouble with bunts. When he is faced with a ground ball, he tends to grab it and fire to first hurriedly, or else he holds the ball too long and comes close to throwing it away.

And so it was asked of the Giants' Joe Amalfitano, after Koufax's no-hit performance at Dodger Stadium: Why didn't the Giants take advantage of Sandy's known weakness? Why didn't they bunt, for base hits, to upset the young man, to weary him with charging down from the mound?

"You can't," Amalfitano said simply. "His fast ball runs right up your bat."

This is the way ballplayers talk. The picture is vivid. A man suddenly shuffles his feet to get a running start, and bunts at a pitched ball, hoping to lay the ball down, rolling slowly, so that he may beat one out. But the ball will not be so easily contained. Not when Koufax throws it. The fast ball comes zooming in and then it leaps, a rising fast ball that jumps over the bat and explodes in the catcher's mitt. Dodger vice-president Fresco Thompson says: "Koufax has more than velocity. His fast ball has a fantastic rise. It seems to take off before reaching the plate and is very hard for a hitter to track."

So instead of bunting, you stand there, dug in, and you take your swings, because this is the age of the home run,

and sometime or other you pray that a swiftly thrown ball will be timed correctly and driven out of sight. Some time or other.

But not too often, when Sandy Koufax pitches. It is the age of the home run, and it is the age of the strikeout, and the irresistible force of the slugger is nicely resisted when Sandy Koufax raises his right leg high in the air, his knee bent, the ball momentarily hidden from sight, behind glove that in turn is behind the leg, and begins the hip-swiveling forward motion, the handsome dark face icily intent, lips thinned and slightly parted, as a baseball prepares to speed homeward. There is beauty to such skill, and Koufax himself expresses it:

"Now I can go out to the mound and not only think about what I should do with each batter, but I can execute my idea most of the time. It's the difference between just playing a game and really knowing a game. It's like one man knowing how to play chess and another man playing chess only because he knows which way the various pieces can be moved."

Sandy Koufax. Chess master. Ruler of the city of the blinded batters.

3

"I Was Scared to Death"

SANDY KOUFAX LIVES in comfort in a two-bedroom-and-den ranch-style house, with a small pool, in Studio City, in the San Fernando Valley, beneath the soft peaks of the Hollywood Hills.

He looks out at the world from behind almost menacing heavy eyebrows. He is traditionally tall, dark, and handsome, a man who must fight a five-o'clock shadow at noon. He dresses neatly, and occasionally nattily, with a fondness for vivid alpaca sweaters. He enjoys listening to the music of classical composers, musical comedy, popular music, and a spattering of jazz.

He reads books, which among some ballplayers is viewed as slightly odd. He is a bachelor—as of this writing—and with a rare show of good taste, he refuses to speak about his dates.

His mother and father live nearby. He has a grandmother in Miami, whom he is able to see every spring training when the Dodgers move to Vero Beach. He has a sister in New York's Westchester County.

He moves serenely through a life that today would appear to hold little threat to his material well-being. Time, of

course, is a threat to any ballplayer, the inevitable threat and victor. Injury is an always-present threat. But ballplayers must shuck such conscious threats, and bury them behind healthy defenses. Koufax may have his moments of naked terror on the mound, but they are more rare than base hits.

He has reached a pleasant pinnacle of life, and today he is able to reap the benefits of high skill and good fortune.

Some of the benefits may seem dubious. At the Hillcrest Country Club in December of 1963, Sandy Koufax was "honored" at a fund-raising charity dinner. The master of ceremonies that evening was George Jessel, and Jessel is the classic ribber among emcees. And so Koufax heard himself that night lauded as "the most important Hebrew athlete since Samson," and he heard Jessel promise: "You'll remember this night, kid, even three or four years from now when you're pitching for Modesto."

But Koufax also heard his teammate Don Drysdale say, that night, "There never has been a fellow more honored or more deservedly so. We wouldn't be where we are without him. Sandy, God bless you. You deserve everything you get."

It has not always been so, and Sandy Koufax does deserve everything he has won. It has been a long, hard victory. Sandy Koufax has come to where he is out of a past where disillusionment was often the keynote. There have been ballplayers who spring into the big leagues, their talents full-blown. For Koufax it has been a terrible grind, an

accumulation of baseball wisdom in the school of hard knocks delivered by harder baseball bats. They say Joe DiMaggio was born to play baseball. They say Willie Mays was born to play baseball. Sandy Koufax was in no way born to play baseball.

He was born—to be specific—in Brooklyn, on December 30, 1935, the son of a lawyer. It was not exactly the most fortunate year history has ever spun off. It was the year Hitler scrapped the Versailles Treaty and called up German youth into the armed forces. It was the year America's finest folk humorist, Will Rogers, and America's leading aviator, Wiley Post, were killed in a fogged-in plane crash near Point Barrow, Alaska. Italy invaded Ethiopia in 1935, and Ethiopia in turn asked the League of Nations to help, and the League instead began to founder.

Huey Long was shot to death in Baton Rouge. An earthquake in Quetta, India, took 60,000 lives. There has never been an earthquake, since, as costly.

In sports, Babe Ruth played his last major-league game, for the Boston Braves, who fired him.

The Cubs—who won 100 games that season (my, how time has flown and things have changed!)—and the Tigers met in the 1935 World Series, and the Tigers won when Goose Goslin singled and manager Mickey Cochrane scored from second base for a 4–3 triumph in the sixth game.

And as the year closed down—a year of depression and death—Sanford Koufax was born. He lived with his parents and his sister and he attended school in the middle-class

neighborhood of Bensonhurst. In his spare time, Sandy played three-man choose-up basketball at a Jewish Community center and on the school playgrounds near Brighton Beach, which in turn is close by Coney Island. His sport was basketball.

"I never played much baseball," Sandy Koufax has since said. "I wasn't even a big baseball fan. I didn't go to Ebbets Field too often. I used to enjoy watching it on TV. It was more comfortable."

But sometimes he would go. When a school group would use its privileges under the G.O. card—the school's General Organization—Sandy would go along "because that way you got out of school early."

At Lafayette High, Koufax was the school's center, captain, and high scorer on the basketball squad. One day the New York Knicks brought a basketball clinic to Lafayette High, and the high schoolers scrimmaged with the big pros. At that time, the Knick team was built around Harry Gallatin—Harry the Horse—a bruising ballplayer who used his six-feet, six-inches and his 220 pounds under the boards in so aggressive a manner he became one of the finest of all rebounders in the National Basketball Association.

It must not be assumed that against high school youngsters, the Knicks went all out. But the fact is, during the brief practice session Sandy Koufax held his own underneath the basket with Gallatin, and—according to sportswriter Steve Gelman, who was there—outbattled him for many a rebound.

"That kid has amazing leap and amazing strength," Harry Gallatin said of young Sandy Koufax. "We'll be coming back for him someday."

Basketball was Koufax's sport, but he did not completely neglect baseball. During the summers, Sandy worked at camps in upstate New York, counseling the youngsters and playing basketball, but every so often he would show up for a sandlot baseball game, playing for the Coney Island Parkviews.

Two men took keen interest in young Sandy. One was Milt Laurie, manager of the sandlot Parkviews when he was not driving a newspaper truck. The other was Jimmy Murphy, a Brooklyn sportswriter.

Sandy was a first baseman. Like most kids, he enjoyed swinging that bat. Unfortunately, though he swung most earnestly, he seldom connected. One day manager Milt Laurie watched the young first baseman throw the ball around the infield.

"Sandy," he said, "with that arm, you should be a pitcher."

So they worked on it patiently.

"Sandy was wild," Laurie recalls, "but you never saw a kid throw the ball any harder than he did." Koufax's own memory confirms Laurie's judgment:

"I struck out lots . . . when I got the ball over the plate."

Sportswriter Jimmy Murphy wandered over to a Coney Island Parkview game one afternoon and watched a tall lean scatter-armed lefty throw baseballs. Immediately he

tipped off the Brooklyn Dodger management to the fifteen-year-old boy's presence. From that day on, the Dodgers kept a flitting eye on Koufax.

There wasn't too much interest within the Koufax household in this version of Baseball Joe. Irving Koufax never saw his son play baseball until he was sixteen. At that time Sandy was wearing a pair of old borrowed spikes, and occasionally asking his parents to buy him a new pair. Irving Koufax couldn't see that it was necessary, until one Saturday he wandered over to Erasmus Field, where his son was playing a ball game. That night Irving Koufax said to his wife, Evelyn:

"Give the boy some money for spikes. You don't want him to break a leg, do you?"

In Sandy's senior year at Lafayette High, he made the baseball team as a first baseman. But he was still a basketball player, and it was as such he won a five-year athletic scholarship to the University of Cincinnati in the fall of 1953. Not that Sandy was an "athletic bum." He went to college because he wanted to become an architect.

Sandy immediately tried out for and made the varsity basketball squad, and helped the team win twelve of fourteen games, averaging ten-plus points per game, in his freshman year. Then, in the spring of 1954, Koufax tried out for the baseball team. Thirty-two innings later, Sandy was 4-and-0, and in those thirty-two innings he had struck out 51 batters. The scouts of several major-league teams had taken an interest in the eighteen-year-old athlete.

In June of 1954, his freshman year behind him, Sandy Koufax appeared at the Polo Grounds in Manhattan, at the request of the New York Giants.

"I was scared to death," Sandy Koufax recalls.

Koufax was handed a baseball. Giant utility man and pinch hitter Bobby Hofman put on the catcher's glove. Giant pitching coach Frank Shellenback stood close by.

Koufax hit the screen behind Hofman with his first pitch. Manager Leo Durocher—busy directing his Giants to a pennant and World Series that season—took a cursory look and hid a grin. Koufax threw steadily, and with unerring inaccuracy. Finally Shellenback patted him on the back and thanked him. That was the last Koufax heard from the Giants.

But just as one no-hitter does not make a career, one wild fling does not break a career. Koufax found himself also invited to try out in Brooklyn, Pittsburgh and Milwaukee. The Dodgers actually asked Sandy to pitch batting practice at Ebbets Field, but it rained that September evening and the grounds keepers threw a tarp over the infield, so Koufax instead threw to catch Rube Walker along the sidelines. Dodger scout Al Campanis, club vice-president and former ballplayer Fresco Thompson, and manager Walter Alston watched. The boy began to fire.

Nobody said a word.

He was wild, though not quite as wild as at the Polo Grounds. Then he finished, and again he was patted on the back. He left, and still nobody had said a pertinent word.

But scout Al Campanis remembers today: "He threw so fast I had a tough time seeing the ball."

Campanis began to visit with the Koufaxes in their home in Bensonhurst. One evening he made a concrete offer. The Dodgers would give Koufax $20,000. The figure broke down into a $14,000 bonus and a first-year salary of $6,000.

The Koufaxes—father and son—discussed the offer. It was hoped that the Pirates or the Braves would top the Dodger bid. So the Koufaxes waited patiently. Then on December 13, 1954, Irving Koufax said to his underage son: "What do you want to do?"

"Let's go ahead and sign," Sandy said. Irving Koufax took Campanis's papers with him to his law office the next morning, studied them closely, and with a small touch of reluctance, signed.

Had the Koufaxes waited a day, they would have been visited by Pittsburgh scout Ed McCarrick, who had been ordered by Pirate general manager Branch Rickey to top any Dodger offer by $5,000. Shortly after, they would have received a $30,000 bid from Milwaukee.

But once again this is playing the chancy game of "If." Had they waited too much longer, and no other bid been forthcoming, the Dodgers might have lost interest.

On December 14, 1954—sixteen days before Sandy's nineteenth birthday—the boy officially became a big-leaguer. It is not a day historians will mark. The news of the world that December 14 was neither more nor less earth-

shaking than the news of other days in this anxious era. There were riots in Cyprus. The State Department denied that any "deal" was in the making with Red China, to expedite the freeing of eleven imprisoned American airmen.

On the sports pages there was baseball news, but again the earth did not shake. Preacher Roe—Dodger left-hander—and veteran third baseman Billy Cox had been sold to the Baltimore Orioles for $55,000. And a boy named Sandy Koufax had signed a bonus agreement with the Dodgers. A handful of teen-aged sports fans in Brooklyn who had seen Sandy play choose-up basketball noted the news item, and one of them said: "I didn't even know he played baseball."

At that time any ballplayer who received more than a $6,000 bonus—Koufax was getting $14,000—had to stay on the roster of the big-league club for the next two seasons, plus thirty days of the third season. It was a rule designed to prevent any one well-heeled organization from signing up all the bright prospects in sight and shipping them down to farm teams for seasoning. This way it was not likely a team would add more than one untried youngster to its limited roster. No team could corner the market in talented kids. The "have" and "have-not" teams were placed on a relatively equal footing.

So Sandy Koufax—embryonic architect and high-scoring basketeer—left the University of Cincinnati and traveled to Florida early in 1955. He did not easily give up the dream of becoming an architect. In 1955 he enrolled at Columbia University for courses. Today, when he speaks of

the future, he says he still toys with the idea of becoming an architect when his baseball career is over.

But that is the future. Let us look back to the year 1955. The ball club Sandy Koufax joined that March is considered by many experts as the finest Dodger team ever assembled. In their authoritative work, *The History of Baseball,* authors Allison Danzig and Joe Reichler, assess the 1955 team.

> The Dodgers that year had the pitching, the hitting, the fielding, and the speed. In a strong league, they were first in scoring runs and first in preventing them. In other words, they had the best offense and the best defense, a surefire formula for success in almost any sport.
>
> The 1955 Dodgers hit more than 200 home runs, the third team in major-league history to exceed 200. They also led the league in stolen bases. It is most unusual to find a team that combines overwhelming power with overwhelming speed. The Brooklyn pitching was the best in the National League. The staff had the lowest earned-run average and it led in strikeouts.

Writer Dan Daniel sums up the 1955 crew succinctly: "Pitching, fight, punch, speed and audacity."

The names are by now legend, among baseball buffs. Hodges, Snider, Campanella, Reese, Gilliam, Furillo and Robinson. Newcombe, Loes, Podres, Erskine, and terrible-tempered Russ Meyer. Its manager was Walter Alston, a

former high school teacher whose major-league playing career lasted exactly one game, one time at bat, and one strikeout, and whose fielding career totaled one putout and one error, all in a game in 1936. His managing career has been better.

The team's spring-training roster numbered 42 men, and of the 42, Sandy Koufax, youngest in age and least in experience, was surely the last man.

For the second time in his life, Sandy Koufax said: "I was scared to death."

He also said: "I'll never forget my first year. I didn't know what I was doing. I had just turned nineteen, and there I was in spring training with the greatest names in baseball—Reese, Snider, Robinson. I had no right being there. They gave me money, and now, every time I threw, I could feel someone watching me. So I tried to throw a little harder just to prove that I was worth the money. I ended up hurting my arm. For two weeks I was combing my hair and brushing my teeth right-handed."

Manager Alston—a patient, silent man as all expert fishermen and bridge players must be, and as managers ought to be, but, alas, often aren't—reveals today what he felt nearly ten years ago. "I couldn't believe my eyes. Playing pepper and tossing the ball back and forth, he was so wild the other fellow couldn't catch it, and when he was just lobbing them to a catcher, three or four out of every twenty pitches would be over the catcher's head."

There was another newcomer to the Dodger camp that

spring, and the two newcomers found themselves thrown together. Out of necessity. The second new man was pitching coach Joseph Edward Becker, a man who spent twenty years as a catcher and nine years managing in the minors before joining the Dodgers. He had once been a teammate of Bob Feller's. Joe Becker instantly sized up a problem which lay beneath the surface. Here was a youngster, on a team made up of old pros. He had mechanical difficulties, as would any untried boy. Becker sensed there had to be mental problems. So the coach hustled the boy behind the barracks at Vero Beach for his daily warm-up, away from prying eyes of fans and players alike.

"You get enough people whispering, 'Wow, is he wild!' and you can ruin a kid," Becker has since explained. "We didn't want to ruin a kid with that kind of arm." And behind the barracks, out of sight, Becker began to analyze the boy, his strengths and weaknesses. Slowly started the process of converting Sandy Koufax, boy wild man, into the mature mound artist of today. On the plus side, Becker said: "Sandy had the right equipment to begin with. He was big, strong, smart, and had a powerful arm, and an eagerness to learn. But—he was a kid with just one summer of sandlot experience and one season of freshman college ball behind him. We had to start from scratch, teaching him to stride, throw with an overhand motion, follow through, snap his wrist, and field his position." And in late summer of 1955, pitching coach Joe Becker made what appears to have been an astonishing prophecy:

"I think Sandy is going to be a great pitcher some day. He has the ability, desire to learn, and a great willingness to cooperate."

Yet it wasn't so astonishing. Koufax could throw. Always, he was the boy with the golden arm. The problem was refinement. The problem was seasoning. The problem was time. But the arm, without which the desire, the willingness, the intelligence would have been useless in the making of a great pitcher, was always there.

Still, the converse may be even more true. With a great arm, but lacking desire, all you have is purposeless muscle. Koufax had the desire.

Perhaps he had a bit too much that first season. He had already strained his arm the first weeks of training. Now, while shagging flies in the outfield before a doubleheader on April 17, 1955, Sandy Koufax sprained his right ankle. He returned to the squad in a few days, and before the game of April 28, while again taking outfield practice, he sprained his left ankle. He sat out a few more days, and when he returned, he threw so hard in the hope of getting quickly back in shape that he hurt his arm again, and was placed on the disabled list for thirty days.

Curiously, what may have made it worse is that the Dodgers actually had no need of Koufax, healthy or ill, those first weeks of the '55 campaign. No team in the history of the league had ever opened a season so well. The Dodgers won their first 10 ball games. They dropped 2 out of 3 to the Giants, and then reeled off a string of eleven

wins, and stood 22-and-2. The remainder of the league, including the World Champion Giants, wallowed in their wake. Duke Snider, Dodger center fielder, got on base in 34 consecutive games. Don Newcombe won 10 games in a row, and put the frosting on the cake by setting off on a home-run hitting binge of his own, eventually breaking the NL record for homers by a pitcher. Behind the plate, handling with consummate skill the deliveries of Newk, Erskine, young John Podres, Russ Meyer, and Billy Loes, was Roy Campanella, headed for his third MVP award.

Koufax? Who's he? Oh, the wild kid with the sore arm. Who needs him?

On Friday, June 24, 1955, manager Walt Alston handed a baseball to one Sanford (Sandy) Koufax after the fourth inning of a ball game in Milwaukee, and sent him out to the mound.

For reasons that attest only to local insanity, there were 43,068 fans in the stands of Milwaukee's County Stadium. Perhaps the reason is that the Braves were in second place.

Fourteen games behind the Dodgers.

But fourteen behind or not, the Milwaukee team that evening was—as it still is—a power-packed lineup. When Sandy Koufax, in a state approaching numbness, glanced in at the hitters he would face in that fifth inning, his first in the big leagues, the men he saw were Johnny Logan, Eddie Mathews, and Henry Aaron.

Behind Aaron would come Bobby Thomson and Joe Adcock. It would have been enough to unsettle an older, wiser hand.

Logan singled.
Mathews walked.
Aaron walked.
Bases loaded. Nobody out.
Bobby Thomson stepped in.

4

"Baseball Isn't Just Peaches and Cream"

BOBBY THOMSON is a symbol to the Dodgers. It is Thomson who hit the home run in the ninth inning of the third game of the 1951 play-off between the Giants and the Dodgers, to drive in three runs, beat Brooklyn, and break Ralph Branca's heart.

But Thomson was more than a Dodger killer. He represented to the Dodgers, and to Dodger fans, the specter of the ever-successful foe, the man who thwarts even the most splendid efforts of the home team. Up until the year 1955, the Brooklyn Dodgers were a team fatally flawed by a character disorder. They suffered from a staggering sense of inferiority. Even in winning—as the Dodgers had won in ten pennants in its National League history up until 1955—the winning was always tinged with a mocking sense of shame. The Dodgers were always the team with two men on third base at the same time. They were the team where a man doubled into a double play, and we conveniently forget that the Dodgers won the ball game that day. They were the team of Babe Herman, fly balls cascading from his shoul-

ders. We forget that Herman was one of the great hitters of National League history. They were the team in 1941 that could have an umpire raise his right arm for the third strike and the third out in the ninth inning of a World Series game, leading 4–3, and still go on to lose, 7–4, as the third strike skipped past Mickey Owen.

They seemed to take pains in celebrating their losses. When the Dodgers played their first night ball game, back on June 15, 1938, a huge and happy throng came out to honor the occasion. What happened? Johnny VanderMeer pitched a no-hitter against Brooklyn.

And when old Ebbets Field had first opened its door back in 1913, it literally didn't open its door. Nobody had the key. When the key was finally located, it was discovered the builder had forgotten to erect a press box. When the teams marched to center field to raise the flag in traditional opening-day ceremonies, it turned out there was no flag.

There was always a brawling, boisterous, almost vulgar quality to the Dodgers that years of winning had not effaced. For even with winning pennants, the Dodgers had never won a World Series. World Series? Who hit into the first and only unassisted triple play in a Series game? A Dodger batter. And who gave up the first bases-loaded home run in a Series game? A Dodger pitcher. Incredibly, and only to Brooklyn could it happen, both occurred in the same game, October 10, 1920.

Ah, it has been a team. Probably the most intriguing team of any sport this nation has ever known. A clawing

team that battled you fiercely, even when it lost, as it most often did lose. A team of incongruity, even of absurdity. They called the team the Trolley Dodgers, which is amusing enough, but they also called them the Superbas, the Daffiness Boys, the Bums, and the Bridegrooms, which is too much. They had an owner and manager, Wilbert Robinson —Uncle Robbie—who in his playing days had once gone seven for seven and had knocked in eleven runs in a single game, but who is best remembered for his inability to manage. Once, as Frank Graham relates in his book, *The Brooklyn Dodgers,* Brooklyn ballplayer Chick Fewster began to bang his bat noisily on the top step of the dugout, to rattle an opposing pitcher.

"Cut that out!" Uncle Robbie ordered.

"Why?" Fewster asked.

Robinson pointed to Dodger pitcher Jess Petty, snoozing in a corner of the dugout. "I don't want to wake old Jess."

When they built a plaque to Uncle Robbie at Ebbets Field, they misspelled his name. What a team!

It was the team of spitballing Burleigh Grimes, Babe Herman, and Frenchy Bordagaray, who wore a mustache. It was the team of poor Hugh Casey who killed himself before alcohol did the job. It was the team of Van Lingle Mungo—they don't hardly make names like that anymore —who tore up clubhouses and once fought Ernest Hemingway with his fists, and knocked him down twice. Van Mungo could throw a baseball through cement, when he felt like it.

It was the team of Dazzy Vance, who had been with 13 teams without winning a single major-league ball game when he joined the Dodgers at the age of thirty-one, and then promptly won 18 games in his first full year.

But mainly and most indelibly it was the team of 1951, leading the second-place Giants by thirteen and a half games on August 10, blowing the lead, and then seemingly regaining it all in the eighth inning of the third play-off game on a gray Wednesday afternoon at the Polo Grounds in October of 1951, leading 4–1.

But the Giants had rallied in the ninth, and out had gone Don Newcombe, that other strange, enigmatic Dodger figure, and in had come young Ralph Branca, and up had come Bobby Thomson, and outbound had gone a baseball, into the left field seats.

Ralph Branca, of course, wore number 13.

Now it was younger Sandy Koufax. Wherever he looked, there were Braves. Logan, Mathews, and Aaron on the bases. Joe Adcock in the on-deck circle.

Bobby Thomson at the plate.

Sandy Koufax took a long, deep breath and wondered why he wasn't learning to be an architect. His baseball house was caving in.

Koufax was a bonus baby. No matter how the Braves bombed him, the Dodgers could not send him down for minor-league seasoning. Not until May of 1957. But on a team romping its way to a pennant, it would have been easy

indeed to forget all about the youngster. Forget him entirely. Why waste Joe Becker's time? There were other kids to be worked on. Surely there would be fewer such appearances as this stint in Milwaukee, unless the boy showed something.

He struck out Bobby Thomson.

Adcock hit into a double play.

In the sixth inning, Koufax registered another strikeout, and the Braves went down in order. Koufax had pitched two scoreless innings of relief, in his first major-league outing.

Five days later, at Ebbets Field, the local fans had a chance to see Koufax. There weren't too many people in the ball park that afternoon, and by the ninth inning, there were far fewer. All because of Willie Mays.

If Bobby Thomson represents a *symbol* to Dodger fans, Willie Mays is the flesh. In more recent years, Dodger pitchers have come to contain Mays, but in the days of Ebbets Field, and the first year of the Los Angeles Coliseum, Mays was a window breaker whenever he saw a Dodger pitcher. In his first 153 games played against the Dodgers, over a span of seven years, Mays hit 59 home runs. And 1955 was the peak. In 11 games played at Ebbets Field that season, Mays hit 9 home runs. It remains a league record for home runs hit in an enemy ball park. You can project away, if you wish. At that rate, Mays would have hit 126 home runs in 1955. (He didn't; all he hit was 51.)

On June 29, 1955, Mays had himself a day.

He hit a bases-empty home run.

He hit a bases-loaded home run.

He singled with a man on third.

Six runs batted in.

He made an incredible catch in center field.

When Sandy Koufax came into the contest, in the ninth inning, the score was Mays 6, Dodgers 0. (In the bottom half of the ninth, the Dodgers would finally score a run.) In the top of the ninth, with Koufax making his second big-league appearance, he pitched a typical Koufax inning. He walked some men, and got some other men out, and finally there were two outs, and the bases loaded, and Willie Mays at bat.

Koufax blew down Mays.

A pattern was developing, a pattern which would last for many years. Young Sandy Koufax was a groping figure on the mound. "I don't think I had pitched more than 100 innings anywhere—sandlot or college freshman—when the Dodgers signed me," Koufax has since related. "I didn't even know how to stand on the mound properly."

Joe Becker had since shown him how to stand on the mound, but knowing how to move the pieces is not the same as chess wisdom. Koufax knew how to stand, but sometimes his mind went blank as he furiously tried to remember all the advice and then blend it all into one strong rhythmic gesture. Sometimes, as if by magic, it worked. Other times, a baseball was thrown out of a welter of arms

and twisting hips, and maybe it went here and maybe it went there, and mainly it just went.

On Wednesday, July 6, 1955, the Dodgers played a twi-night doubleheader at Pittsburgh's Forbes Field. Forbes Field is a pitcher's field. The fences are far removed. Left-handers especially enjoy working in Pittsburgh, because—with right-handed hitters stacked against them—that distant left field fence is a distinct comfort. Not that the ball can't be driven out. It can. Ask Bill Mazeroski. Or, if you dare, ask Ralph Terry. Still, it *is* a "fur piece," and in this friendly acreage, and after the Dodgers had won the twilight portion of the doubleheader, manager Alston handed Sandy Koufax his first starting assignment. The Pirates finished eighth that year, as they had finished eighth for each of the previous three years. They were—at the time—one of the worst teams ever to play in the National League. The only real talent in the organization lay in the office of vice-president. This was Harry L. Crosby, better known as Bing.

Still, they were major-leaguers, good or bad, and they were facing a boy who later admitted he was "nervous, and brother, that's the understatement of the year."

Before a crowd of 20,374, Sandy Koufax sweated that night. In four and two-thirds innings, he made 106 pitches. He walked eight men and struck out four, and yielded three hits. Still, there was the pattern. Men would clog the bases, and suddenly Koufax would turn around and get them out. With eight walks and three hits in four-plus innings, the Yankees used to win pennants. This was not the Yankees.

This was Pittsburgh. Eight walks and three hits in less than five innings—and just one run. When Alston finally removed the fatigued youngster, the score stood 1–1. Ed Roebuck came in, and the Pirates went on to win, 4–1, behind Vernon Law. Roebuck took the loss.

Alston kept spoon-feeding the boy into ball games. No more starts for a while. Even the relief appearances were rare.

"The first year was very frustrating," Sandy Koufax has since told *Sport* magazine writer Steve Gelman. "We'd be six or seven runs behind, and I'd get up in the bullpen and start throwing. Then say we'd rally a little, maybe get two or three runs back. Well, I'd sit right down again. It got so I wasn't sure if I had made the right decision, quitting college to come into baseball. But I figured, well, it was a good way to make a living, and that eased things a trifle."

But not much. Whenever Koufax made an appearance, it would be in a game that was knocked out of sight, beyond even the power-hitting Dodgers' ability to coax back. And so, six or seven runs behind, and not rallying at all, and nothing to do but play out the string and trot out the roster, Alston would send in his youngster, Sandy Koufax.

Then on Saturday, August 27, at Ebbets Field, Koufax made his second start.

This time it was not the Pirates. It was the Cincinnati Reds, perhaps the sluggingest team in the league. Up and down the lineup, there was the home-run threat. Ted Kluszewski and Wally Post would each hit over 40 home

runs in 1955. On July 29, both Bob Thurman and Smoky Burgess would hit bases-loaded home runs. Earlier that year, the Reds had hit 5 home runs in one game—two by Ray Jablonski, one each by Andy Seminick, Thurman, and Post. There wasn't much else it could or would do—Cincinnati finished fifth that year—but the team could hit. And especially in Ebbets Field, with its intimate fences.

In the second inning, big Ted Kluszewski hit a ground ball through the hole to right field, for a single.

With two out in the ninth, Sam Mele drilled a double to left center.

That was it.

Sandy Koufax pitched a two-hitter. He struck out 14 batters. He fanned Gus Bell—who earlier that season had hit three home runs in one game—four times. The Dodgers won, 7–0.

Sandy ran into trouble only once. With one out in the sixth inning, he walked Johnny Temple and Burgess. And out of the dugout came Walter Alston—running—to pacify the youngster.

"I told him not to aim the ball," Alston said. "I told him to keep throwing hard."

The manager understood the temptation. You walk a man and then another, and you start worrying. What happens if you walk a third, and the bases are loaded, and then the next man catches hold of one, and there go four runs? So instead of adhering to your natural rhythm, to the pattern that had worked so beautifully through five and a third

innings, you freeze with fear, and you deliberately try to throw a baseball over the plate. If there is a definition of a gopher ball, you have just read it.

Koufax kept throwing, not aiming. He got out of the inning, and out of the seventh and eighth, and then with two out, Mele doubled, and the shutout was up for grabs in the ninth inning.

Koufax forced himself not to think in terms of shutouts, or even of victories. He thought of the hitter, and how best to pitch to him. He came whipping in with his fast balls, and the batter, Rocky Bridges, hit a meek pop fly to short, where Pee Wee Reese gathered it in.

Sandy Koufax had won his first big-league game, had pitched his first complete game, had rung up his first shutout, and in the process had struck out more men than any other National League pitcher would strike out in a single game that year. Sam Jones and Buhl had struck out twelve. Bill Loes had fanned eleven.

With one ball game, he had entered the record books.

Not just once. Four Cincinnati pitchers that afternoon had struck out nine Dodgers. The two-team total—23—tied a major-league record, set first by the Braves and Reds in 1901, equaled by the Yankees and Senators in 1914, and again tied later in 1955.

"It was a wonderful feeling," Koufax has since said. But not entirely wonderful. "As I look back at it now, that game may have hurt more than it helped. I threw real hard in the

game, and it worked. I threw much harder than I should have, and it took me a long time to learn that it was wrong."

It may have been wrong in other ways. Suddenly—without a moment's warning—the boy was big news. Up until that afternoon, there were baseball fans who didn't even know how to pronounce Sandy's last name. Was it Koofax or Kohfax or Kowfax? I remember listening to an earlier Giant-Dodger game in 1955, and hearing of a relief pitcher named Koufax, and I realized that up until then I had never heard of the youngster.

Now we all heard of him. There was his picture, big as life, in the paper. We learned that he wore 32 on his back. That he roomed with Billy Loes on the road. (We all knew of Loes, one-time bonus baby with a boisterous, Dodgerish manner, a pitcher who swore he'd lost a ground ball in the sun, in the 1953 World Series.)

Reporters pressed Koufax, to squeeze out what color and what news there was in the boy. Koufax squeezed color badly in those days; he squeezes not much better today. Color him neutral. It turned out that the boy's biggest thrill was watching his father write. Irving Koufax was ambidextrous. Not only could he write with either hand, but he could actually write from left to right with his right hand, and right to left with his left hand, making the letters backward. All at the same time!

But the name of the game is baseball, not penmanship. Sandy Koufax started two more games that 1955 season.

Milwaukee batted him out of the box in one inning.

He turned around and shut out the Pirates with a five-hitter. He struck out six.

When the season had ended, Koufax's record stood at two wins, two losses. He'd been in twelve games, a total of 42 innings. He struck out 30 men—and walked 28. He gave up 33 hits. His earned-run average was a surprising 3.00. It would not again be so low until 1962.

Sketchy as they are, and bolstered by hindsight, the 1955 statistics furnish a profile of the Sandy Koufax baseball fans were to come to know for the next five years. Like the girl in the nursery rhyme, when he was good, he was very very good. When he was bad, he was horrid.

But it had been more than just a few innings of pitching. It had been a year of learning, in the crucible of a pennant race, and when it was over, Koufax had learned much. He had learned that his own biggest problem was control. He even had some advice for other youngsters hoping to break into baseball.

"Start as early as you can," said Koufax in the fall of 1955 in an interview with Herman L. Masin, sports editor of *Senior Scholastic* magazine. "Learn as much as you can. Study the good pitchers. Try to get the advice of a good coach. Don't fool around with freak pitches. They can come later."

And, feverishly repeating it as a catechism:

"Develop that *control*."

The boy had matured, a bit. He had come into baseball, as has nearly every rookie, with dreams of glory, with

dreams of a life that would be pure gold. Gold and fun and fame. Baseball—then—was a game.

In one short year, it had become a business.

"Baseball isn't just peaches and cream," Koufax warned Masin. "It's mostly bread and butter."

5

"Are You That Much of a Fan?"

NO MAN IS AN ISLAND, the poet tells, and no single ballplayer is sufficient unto himself. The story of Sandy Koufax, baseball player extraordinary, must also be the story of the Dodgers, ball team incredible, from 1955 to the present day. We are molded by our environment, and a ballplayer's environment, other than airline seats and hotel lobbies and the awful majestic loneliness of the mound or the batter's box, is the team. Sandy Koufax pitched 42 innings in 1955. The team played over 1,400 innings. Koufax won 2 games. The Dodgers won 98. What went on on the field helped make Sandy Koufax what he is today.

He joined a team that was a winner. Had he joined the Phillies or the Pirates, everything that has followed would have been, to a degree, different. This is not to say a losing team cannot list a great player on its roster. It can and often does. But no matter what, he wasn't on the Phils or the Pirates or even the third-place Giants. He was a Dodger. A winner. The most overpowering single baseball team the National League has ever fielded.

No team ever clinched a National League pennant as

early as the 1955 Dodgers. On September 8, the Dodgers beat Milwaukee, 10–2, and boosted their lead to 17 games. The magic number was reduced to zero.

Still, these were the Dodgers. Had a Yankee team won a pennant by 13½ games—the margin by which the Dodgers would win—it would have put a final ho-hum to the whole dreary affair. The Dodgers were in first place for 166 days of the 168-day season, and missed those two days only because the Cubs opened a day earlier, and won, and the Dodgers' own opener was rained out. Otherwise, it was the Dodgers, all the way. Yet somehow it was never dreary.

They were the Dodgers, scrapping—this time—among themselves. Jackie Robinson battled with manager Alston, complaining that he wasn't being played enough. Campanella griped that he didn't like batting eighth. Newcombe didn't want to pitch batting practice, and, in fact, refused to do so twice in the same week. Alston suspended him. Newcombe went home to Jersey City, and then returned to apologize. In his next start, Newk yielded one hit to Chicago, and faced exactly 27 batters. Snider—the All-Star center fielder—had a superb season, driving in a league-leading 136 runs, hitting a club record of 42 home runs. So? So the Dodger fans booed him lustily late in August when Snider left eight runners on base in the first game of a doubleheader. And Snider bellowed back: "Fans! What a bunch of crummy front-runners! They're the worst fans in the league. They don't deserve a pennant. We're fighting to win the pennant. I hope to hell we move to Jersey!"

Dodgers.

And Sandy Koufax was one of them. Not that you'd ever have known it. He was, then, a painfully shy boy. When nobody was looking that year, he signed for a night class in architecture at Columbia University. One evening in September, just after the Dodgers had clinched the pennant, he asked his instructor for permission to cut class so that he might attend the team's victory party.

The instructor said: "Are you that much of a fan?"

"Not exactly," Koufax answered. "I'm on the team."

"I never would have known," the instructor murmured.

Nobody would have known. Still, it was a fact, and as the Dodgers went, so went Sandy. Into the 1955 World Series. He didn't pitch a single inning. Nobody figured he would. Yet he was part of the Series, as was every man on each roster.

The Dodgers had never won a Series. Always, it had been: "Wait 'till next year!"

If ever a "next" year appeared to be in the offing, it was this year. The Yankees had been decimated by injuries. Casey Stengel had juggled his lineup like an India-rubber ball, and the club had staggered in, three games ahead of the Indians. It was an odd club. The second baseman, Billy Martin, had just come out of service. The two aces, Whitey Ford and Bob Turley, were fine, healthy pitchers, but after that, there were only question marks. Ed Lopat had dropped off to a 7-and-12 record. Young Bob Grim had a sore arm. Don Larsen, who had lost 21 games the previous year with

Baltimore, and who also had a sore arm, was just recently experimenting with a new windup-less delivery. He'd stand on the mound, his hands together at his belt, and then he'd throw the ball to the plate. Odd. You'd think a Dodger would have invented it.

There was power aplenty, of course. After all, these still were the Yankees. Mantle, Skowron, and Hank Bauer maced opposing pitchers all season long, and Yogi Berra continued to hit home runs when they counted until he, too, won his third Most Valuable Player award.

Perhaps the oddest Yankee on that good-and-bad team was an erratic thirty-six-year-old left-hander named Tommy Byrne. Byrne was an old man, as players go, when this 1955 World Series hove to. He'd pitched in the 1949 Series, but soon after, his inability to throw strikes, and a lame back, had induced the Yankees to unload the southpaw. Why not? In the three prior seasons, Byrne had walked 179 men (a Yankee record), 160, and 150. One game he hit 4 batters. Another time he walked 16. He always had oodles of stuff: a live fast ball, a sharp curve, and—late in his career, a nifty slider—but the problem was where to put the stuff.

The Yankees solved the problem by putting it all on the St. Louis Brown roster. The Browns sent it to the White Sox, who dittoed it to Washington who put it down in Charleston, in the American Association, from whence it traveled to the winter league in the Caribbean and then to Seattle, in the Pacific Coast League. Here Charley Dressen

saw Byrne and suggested to Yankee executive George Weiss that he get all that stuff back, because travel had somehow refined the raw spots in Byrne. So George Weiss rescued Byrne, and brought the big man, six-one and 187 pounds, back to the Yankees where he pitched and no longer just threw.

If you are guessing that there is something similar in Byrne to the Sandy Koufax story, you're probably right. Tommy Byrne never became a master of control (as Sandy Koufax may indeed become), and Byrne was never quite the stuff pitcher Koufax was and is. But there are more similarities than differences—great raw talent, wildness, and a struggle to refine the talent and conquer the wildness.

In 1955, the first year Sandy Koufax played major-league ball, Tommy Byrne concluded the fight. Successfully. Again, he never scored a decisive knockout over his old foe, the base on balls. But it was nicely contained, neatly pocketed, never again to bother Byrne badly. Byrne won 16 ball games and lost 5, and when the Yankees needed to be righted after a few losses, Tommy Byrne stepped in with the stopper-type win. Byrne's ERA that season was 3.15, and he walked "only" 88 men, the first time he'd ever been under 100.

And so as the 1955 World Series swung into action, a nineteen-year-old boy who had averaged six walks for every nine innings he'd pitched was able to watch a man, nearly twice his age, who was ending a struggle against wildness

the boy was just entering. It was a swift glance at the future.

There was a lot of outside looking available to Koufax that year. You could scarcely miss it in the papers. A very wild-armed pitcher named Sam Jones had pitched the lone no-hitter of 1955, walking seven men in the process, including the first three batters to come up in the ninth inning (before striking out the next three).

And a bonus baby named Herb Score, left-handed as all get out, had made his rookie year one of the most memorable on record. Score had won 16 games, while losing 10. Koufax had pitched a two-hitter? Score had a one-hitter. He struck out 245 batters, most ever by a freshman pitcher. His earned-run average was a slim 2.85. But he also walked 153 men. Ah, these swift young left-handers.

At Series time, Sandy Koufax sat in the dugout, and occasionally in the bullpen, but mostly he watched. The Yankees had won their last seven World Series; the Dodgers had lost all seven of theirs, beginning in 1916 when the Red Sox beat them four out of five, and a big moonfaced left-hander—naturally—whipped them in a tense fourteen-inning second game, 2–1. The left-hander was Babe Ruth.

So it was a loser against a winner, and the odds favored the Yankees. Still, there was more than just hope riding on the Dodgers. They were a tremendous team, with a pitching staff headed by Newcombe, and backed up by Carl Erskine, Billy Loes, Podres, Roger Craig, Russ Meyer, and other lesser lights, such as Karl Spooner, who had broken in the

year before with two consecutive shutouts, one of them a 15-strikeout job against the Giants. Then there were Don Bessent, Clem Labine, and Ed Roebuck.

Koufax sat. The supremely confident Yankees beat the Dodgers the first two games, both at the Stadium, 6–5 behind Ford, and 4–2 as Tommy Byrne bested Loes, Bessent, Spooner, and Labine. Byrne was the story. He tossed a five-hitter, walked five, but struck out six, and it was his single in the fourth inning that knocked in two runs and provided the difference.

As a Dodger said: "What a crummy road trip!"

It was the Series of the left-hander. Newcombe, the big right-hander, would not win a game. Ford and Byrne had won the first two. Now young Podres got the Dodgers going, and then right-handers Labine, in relief, and Craig made it a three-game sweep at Ebbets Field before the lefties went to work again at that paradise of left-handers, Yankee Stadium.

No team had ever won a Series after dropping the first two. Now the Dodgers were leading, 3–2. But Ford pitched a beaut, a four-hitter, and the Yankees routed lefty Spooner.

It was Podres against Byrne in the finale, and you know all about it, young Podres beating the old man, 2–0.

Sandy Koufax, bonus baby, a boy not yet twenty years old, a boy who just a year before was wondering miserably whether his wildness in those four tryouts had finished him off for good, was a member of the World Champion Brooklyn Dodgers. The Dodgers had used ten separate

pitchers in the grueling seven-game struggle, and Koufax had been none of them. But it didn't matter. He was a winner, a winner in his first year, and it may have marked him as much as anything that has happened to him in baseball.

The year Sandy Koufax joined the Dodgers was also the year the team at long last buried its inferiority complex, and the snarling, bickering, brawling Dodgers slowly began to take on a new look. Not that the Dodgers no longer brawl. They do, and they still do among themselves. So do other teams. Which is the difference today. When you see a dirty uniform trouser today, you do not assume this has been a Dodger wrestling in the dirt with a Cub or a Giant or with his teammate. It's probably just Maury Wills, who has stolen second, third, and a ball game.

Baseballs still cascade down the bodies of Dodger outfielders—Frank Howard reminds you of Babe Herman—and there they were in the 1963 World Series, two Dodgers on third base at one and the same moment, but it is not the mark of the team. The mark of the team is the strikeout, the double play, the steal, the neatly operated hit-and-run. The mark of the team is intelligence, wit, sophistication, coolness.

The mark of the team is the poise of relief pitcher Ron Perranoski, the cool look and demeanor of Ron Fairly, organization man. These Dodgers play bridge. Those Dodgers played hooky.

It did not all occur because Sandy Koufax joined the

team, but it began in 1955. A quiet shy young man, with a piece of college education, an ambition that runs to architecture, and taste that occasionally arpeggios to Rachmaninoff, came to the Dodgers in 1955, and a World Series was won, and you can make of the coincidence what you will.

Probably just that. Coincidence.

A ballplayer is influenced by more than his teammates. When he is part of the Brooklyn Dodgers, he is a piece of an organization that has all the titles of boards of directors of big corporations. Presidents and vice-presidents and executive secretaries, and young ladies to answer the phone and take dictation. In his first year, Sandy Koufax figured that baseball is not peaches and cream, but bread and butter. Actually, it is dollars and cents. In 1955, the Brooklyn Dodgers finished the most successful financial five-year span in the history of baseball. The team accrued a profit of $1,800,000.

No other team in either league had netted so huge a profit in any five-year period as had the Dodgers, 1951–1955. It says so in the records collected by Representative Emanuel Celler when he and a congressional committee looked into a possible antitrust suit against baseball's management.

But already forces were at work to disrupt this financial success. The park which housed the Dodgers was Ebbets Field, one of the older ball fields in America, an intimate arena seating 32,111, except when the fire department

wasn't looking, as it wasn't looking on May 30, 1934, a doubleheader against the Giants, and 41,209 crammed into the stadium that was surrounded by Bedford Avenue, Sullivan Place, McKeever Place, and Montgomery Street.

But even 41,209 people did not make for a huge baseball crowd, not in comparison with the lordly Yankees up in the Bronx, or even the hated Giants, on the Harlem River. Connie Mack Stadium, in Philadelphia, had a larger seating capacity than Ebbets Field. It was a musty old field, an anachronism in this day of the new Dodger, in this era of World Series winners. From 1955 to 1963, the Dodgers would play in four World Series, and win three of them. Ebbets Field could not contain a team with this future.

Nor could the borough of Brooklyn. The neighborhood surrounding Ebbets Field was a crumbling environs, old buildings and older tenants, coated over with the smell of overflowing garbage and unwashed vestibule walls. People with money or with expectations were leaving the old buildings, and poorer people moved in.

President of the Dodgers, a genial lawyer named Walter F. O'Malley, decided the team must move out of this unlaved neck of a deteriorating city.

The intent—always—was to move West. There were feints in the direction of Jersey City, and feints in the direction of more spacious areas of Brooklyn and Long Island and Queens, but these were plays to win greater concessions while the team stayed in Brooklyn and until the club was ready to declare its move. A ball club does not move over-

night; and what Walter O'Malley wanted would not be built in a day. He wanted a brand-new commodious stadium; he wanted financial concessions that would assure him not only a continued profit, but an even greater profit than the one he and his club had just realized. O'Malley was surely thinking of what had happened when the Boston Braves moved to Milwaukee and began to attract seasonal crowds of two million and more. Baseball is a game children play, but it is a business grown men invest in. Walter Francis O'Malley is the wisest investor baseball has ever known.

This is not to say O'Malley and O'Malley alone is responsible for the success of the Dodgers. If O'Malley is the shrewdest financial man in baseball, his vice-president and general manager, Emil (Buzzie) Bavasi is generally conceded to be the best handler of personnel and the inner workings of a ball team. Bavasi, a smallish peppy balding man who served under Larry MacPhail and Branch Rickey before O'Malley, became executive v-p in 1951 at the age of thirty-five. In the first thirteen years following his appointment, the Dodgers won six pennants.

Nor does it stop with Bavasi. The Dodgers have another vice-president, named Fresco Thompson, former big-league infielder. Thompson is the director of the Dodgers' minor-league activities, and he brings to the job not only his own playing experience, but perhaps the keenest wit of any man in the game. Thompson is also a wise businessman. One year Thompson arranged the purchase by the Dodgers of the Reading club, of the International League, and all its

assets, including a 21-passenger bus, 40 uniforms, and the contracts of 18 players, all for $5,000. One of the 18 players was Carl Furillo, who soon became one of the finest right fielders in the league.

Sandy Koufax is part of all this, too. The machinations of a front office involve all the men, right down to the bat boy. The Dodger organization, headed by that front office, is a crisply efficient structure, versed as much in real estate values and taxes as it is in the double play.

Slowly, the whole organization began to move westward. Even in Los Angeles—the city of the blind—you could see the move starting.

Los Angeles was the ideal place for a new big-league team. Air travel had reduced the one huge obstacle, the problem of transporting two teams from the East Coast to the West Coast for a three- or four-game series, and then flying one or both teams back east again.

The city had tried in the past to lure in other teams. The St. Louis Browns—most western of all baseball cities—announced they would come to Los Angeles in 1941, but Pearl Harbor intervened. With restricted travel and restrictions on building, the move was abandoned. Later, the Browns and Athletics indicated interest in Los Angeles. In 1955, a $4,500,000 bond issue to erect a big-league park in Los Angeles failed, but in the failure, it did not go unnoticed that the people of L.A. were thinking big, four-and-a-half-million-dollars big. They also were thinking in

terms of making a city attractive to a newcomer, instead of waiting for the newcomer to woo it.

Calvin Griffith of the Washington Senators began to extend feelers to the Los Angeles city fathers in 1956, and in April of 1956—as the Dodgers opened its first season as defending World Champions—Walter O'Malley began to wonder aloud whether there was any real future in Brooklyn. He was frankly unhappy about the field he played in, the neighborhood in which it stood, or leaned, and the profits he could eke out in days ahead. And when Los Angeles heard these grumbles from the Dodger office, it was no longer interested in Cal Griffith and his lowly Senators. You don't settle for dolphins when you can gaff the big whale itself.

Nor was this a secret. The emotional outburst from an embittered Duke Snider in August of 1955—"I hope to hell we move to Jersey!"—was an expression of the club's intentions. The question wasn't whether or when the Dodgers would leave Ebbets Field, but where they would head.

Meanwhile, back in the dugout, the game went on. The one called baseball.

If the Dodgers expected to ride easily to a second successive pennant on last year's smashing triumph, they were in for a rude shock. There was nothing easy about the '56 pennant race. The Braves, new emerging power of the league, led for 126 days, the Dodgers for only 17. But, as the Dodgers themselves had learned in 1951 and would see confirmed in 1962, it only counts who leads that last day.

It was a snarling race. The Braves were young and scrappy. The Dodgers were slowly starting to age. Hodges, Furillo, Campy, Reese, and Robinson were all over thirty, and Snider would be thirty in September of 1956. Perhaps a touch of rare overconfidence afflicted Brooklyn through patches of the season. Still, it was an interleague trade, for an aging, seemingly washed-up pitcher, concluded just before the May deadline, that eventually won the pennant for Brooklyn.

Sal Maglie, that old Dodger destroyer, and now thirty-nine years old, came to Brooklyn from Cleveland, where the Indians had found him wanting. It was another experience for the still-young, still-learning Sandy Koufax.

For over a year, Koufax had heard the bristling, sometimes profane remarks by the Dodgers directed against Sal Maglie. Maglie, the Barber. The man who made the brush-back pitch a wicked weapon in setting Dodger hitters back on their heels, and then clipping the outside corner with his magnificent curve. Maglie, the dark-bearded scowling man on the mound, a man who seemed to hate each hitter with a consuming burning hate. And who was hated back.

Later, Sandy Koufax was to say, with a big-leaguer's cynicism:

"A dirty player is the guy who's on the other team. When he joins your side his reputation changes miraculously. Sal Maglie is the perfect example. When Maglie was with the New York Giants, the Dodgers thought his brushback pitching was the most rotten thing we'd ever seen. Carl Furillo

was the angriest Dodger of all. Then Maglie was traded to the Dodgers. We promptly found him to be a wonderful guy and a great help to young pitchers. And his best friend on the Dodgers soon became—Carl Furillo."

You can scrape away the psychology and the cynicism, and get down to the bedrock of fact. Sandy Koufax learned a lesson. In baseball, it is winning that counts. If you stay within the bounds of the rules and the less-clear bounds of decency, you do everything you can to win. One of the most moral of Dodgers, and one of the finest gentlemen ever to play ball, was Gil Hodges. Yet during the years Koufax was with the Dodgers, Gil Hodges was one of the most aggressive base runners in the game, a man whose savage slides rode many a second baseman or shortstop out of a double play and left him sprawled on the ground, blasted loose of the ball.

Maglie was a great help to young pitchers. Sandy Koufax now had a new, older, wiser pitcher to study. Maglie's fast ball had lost its zip; sometimes the great curve refused to bend; his stamina was hampered by a lame back. Yet Maglie—in 1956—was a master, a man who picked at the corners, kept the ball knee-high or tight at the fists, worked inside and then out, and showed Sandy Koufax how far a man could go even when his arm was brass, not golden, and when his stuff simply wasn't there. In the face of adversity, Maglie called on courage. It was a lesson Koufax would someday have to live through himself.

Koufax, pitching only slightly more often in 1956,

watched in fascination. Today Koufax says it no longer thrills him when he pitches superbly and wins. "If a man has good stuff," Koufax has said, "he should win." But Sandy does get a thrill when he does not have good stuff, when—for whatever the reason—his curve ball is not behaving, or his fast ball refuses to take off or sink and instead is a straight line right at a bat, and still he gets the hitters out.

In 1956, Koufax got into 16 games, pitched a total of fifty-nine innings. He won two and lost four. His strikeout total was again 30, but this meant Sandy was striking out men at a less impressive rate than in 1955. Now it was one man every two innings. He gave up twice as many hits in 1956, and his earned-run average was well up, to a mediocre 4.88.

But there is one category in which Koufax showed improvement, and perhaps it is the most important category of all for this golden-armed, scatter-armed boy who was still not old enough to vote. In 1955, Koufax had walked 28 men in forty-two innings, 6 men for every nine innings. In 1956, Koufax walked 29 men in fifty-nine innings, and the average was now fewer than 4½ men per nine-inning game.

Hindsight tells us this was not the beginning of a downward and steady arc, a continuingly successful struggle against wildness. Wildness would recur. But now there was hope the boy would someday be able to place a curve where he wanted it, zip in a fast ball where catcher Campanella or Roseboro would set his glove.

It was not a good year for Koufax. He knew it. He said:

"I tried to strike out a hitter before he got up to the plate. I was destroying myself by throwing too hard."

But you could see that the boy was no longer an even bet to hit the grandstand screen on the fly.

The pressure was on Koufax in 1956 more than it had been in 1955. In '55, the Dodgers were never headed. A more leisurely trial season could not have been invented. On the other hand, 1956 was a dog fight. Any game Koufax was tossed into was a game that counted. The dogfight quality of baseball extended beyond Brooklyn. Ted Williams spat at the fans, and was fined $5,000. Charlie Grimm was fired by Milwaukee because—allegedly—he let his players walk all over him. Then, under new manager Fred Haney, there would be cries the players had choked up in the last days of the race.

In a dogfight, the man with the razor-fine pitches—Sal Maglie—was at his best. On September 11, Maglie beat Milwaukee's Bob Buhl, 4–2, and the Dodgers were tied with the front runners. The Dodgers slipped back, and on Tuesday, September 25, Maglie got them back up there, with a no-hitter against the Phillies, the oldest man to pitch a no-hitter since forty-one-year-old Cy Young beat the Yankees back in 1908.

But Don Newcombe lost the next day, and the Dodgers were a game behind, with three to go, and it rained the next day in Brooklyn while men and boys bit their nails and listened to their radios that finally told them the Braves had

been beaten in St. Louis, 5–4. On Saturday, September 29, Maglie and Labine hurled the Dodgers to a doubleheader win, and that night Warren Spahn pitched twelve innings and gave up but five hits, but the Cardinals beat Milwaukee, 2–1, and the Dodgers had a game lead. They held it.

Sandy Koufax again did not throw a ball in the World Series, but he was part of it. What a Series it was. The big winner, Newcombe, was twice ripped by Yankee bats and perhaps by his own inner torment. Maglie beat Ford in the opener; the second game was a slugfest, the Dodgers winning 13–8, Duke Snider getting the big blow, a three-run home run off the old lefty, Tommy Byrne.

But the big game was the fifth, the two teams tied, 2–2, and Don Larsen going against the crafty Maglie. Maglie pitched with stubborn skill that afternoon, yielding but two runs, and stymieing several Yankee rallies with his gritty clutch pitching. But it was in vain, as would have been just about any pitching performance in the history of the game. Don Larsen threw his perfect game, retiring 27 Dodgers on 97 pitches, and again Koufax was present when history—baseball's and his own—was being made.

In the finale, the Yankees slaughtered Newcombe, the 27-game winner. The score was 9–0. The Dodgers were no longer champions.

All the while, the game of baseball's musical chairs continued. In 1956, while the Dodgers were drawing a million-plus fans for the twelfth successive year, Walter O'Malley sold Ebbets Field to a real estate man for $3,000,000, and then leased the park through 1959. In 1956, the Dodgers

played an experimental seven "home" games at Jersey City's Roosevelt Stadium and drew 148,000 fans. Now O'Malley scheduled eight games in Jersey City for 1957. For all the world, O'Malley was a man with an itch to travel.

But the two games—the one on the field and the other in the locked rooms of businessmen—are dovetailed, and Walter O'Malley sensed what few baseball men were prepared for: the on-field collapse of his Dodgers. For eight years, the Dodgers had either won or finished second. But elements of the team were aging. The Braves were coming on. There were other incipient powers in the league. The Pirates, down in the depths, were starting to stir.

O'Malley knew he had to get out of Brooklyn while he was still a winner, or close to a winner. He had a team with star names. Men who would attract huge audiences in any new city. Hodges and Snider were fabled home-run hitters. Campanella—crippled in 1956 with a bad hand—was still the premier catcher in baseball. Carl Erskine had thrown two no-hitters in his career, one of them just the past June.

But if the team started to sag, the trading value would be tarnished. He had to get out while he could still negotiate from strength.

On February 1, 1957, Phil Wrigley sold his Los Angeles franchise and Wrigley Field—the L. A. version—to O'Malley for $2,500,000. In turn, O'Malley transferred to Wrigley's Cubs the Dodger rights to a minor-league farm in Fort Worth, Texas. In Los Angeles, Mayor Norris Poulson and Los Angeles county supervisor Kenneth Hahn led a junket to Vero Beach, to confer with O'Malley about the possible

sale of a chunk of Los Angeles real estate known as Chavez Ravine.

And before the year was through, the Dodgers had made it official; they weren't going to Jersey City after all. Nor were the Giants headed for Minneapolis. The most lucrative rivalry in baseball would simply transfer its base to California, the Giants in San Francisco, the Dodgers in Los Angeles.

On the face of it, the announcement wasn't a minute too soon. The Dodgers finished third in 1957, eleven games behind pennant-winning Milwaukee. The Giants were sixth, seven games out of the cellar.

The Dodgers made their last appearance at Ebbets Field on September 24, 1957. Organist Gladys Goodding played "California, Here I Come," "After You've Gone," and "Thanks for the Memory." Gil Hodges made the last Dodger out, striking out to close down the eighth inning. The Dodgers won, 2–0.

On October 7, 1957, the Los Angeles City Council approved by a 10–4 vote a contract with the Dodgers to play ball in Los Angeles in 1958. The next day, O'Malley wired Mayor Poulson:

> GET YOUR WHEELBARROW AND SHOVEL. I'LL MEET YOU AT CHAVEZ RAVINE.

In the weeks of politicking, the individual exploits of second-echelon ballplayers tended to be passed over in

1957. Yet 1957 was a pivotal year in the career of Sandy Koufax.

His bonus restriction had kept him on the Dodger roster through 1956 and into 1957. After that, it was up to him to stick. Koufax stuck.

The slow learning process was starting to make itself felt. They still called on Koufax infrequently, but his name no longer made you frown and say: Koufax? Koufax? Let's see, he's that bonus kid, isn't he? How's he doing?

People knew.

Koufax appeared in 34 games, in a 154-game season, which means you were seeing the young man better than once every five days. He pitched 104 innings, more than he had pitched in his first two years together. He won 5 games and lost 4, which still indicates little, but in 1957, Koufax had begun to zero in on the strike zone. Not just aiming the ball. Powering it through. In 104 innings, Koufax struck out 122 men. It is an eye-popping statistic. Better than a man an inning. Better than 10 men per nine-inning game.

It is a recurrent figure with Koufax. It is a figure he, alone, claims. No other starting pitcher in the history of the game has ever struck out a man an inning, except in an occasional game. Koufax has struck out better than a man an inning throughout his career. Walter Johnson didn't do it. Bob Feller didn't do it. Dizzy Dean didn't do it. Don Drysdale isn't going to do it.

Only Koufax.

For a brief spell, it appeared that Koufax might put

together a decent number of wins. When Sandy pitched a four-hitter in Chicago on August 1, 1957, to beat the Cubs, 12–3, Sandy's record stood at five wins, two losses. With two whole months to go, it did not seem inconceivable that Koufax would put together a ten-win season; perhaps he might even win twelve.

Unfortunately, he did not win another game. He was knocked out of the box in Pittsburgh in the fifth inning, on August 17, losing the game, 7–3. True, he had struck out 6 men in less than five innings, but he had also walked 4 men, and the Pirates had tagged him with men on base.

Koufax did not start again until September 10, again in Chicago, but this time the Cubs jumped all over him, and rookie Dick Drott beat Brooklyn, 10–2.

It was relief the rest of the way. And Koufax seemed to find himself again. He pitched well on Sunday, September 15, in Cincinnati, but the Dodgers were clobbered, 11–6. He pitched well in relief five days later, but the Dodgers lost, 3–2. He pitched in Philadelphia a week later, giving up no hits in one inning, but his team lost again, 3–2, as rookie Jack Sanford won his nineteenth. And then, on the last day the Dodgers would represent Brooklyn—September 29, 1957—Koufax again pitched a perfect inning of relief. The Dodgers lost to Seth Morehead and the Phils, 2–1.

The season ended; an era ended. So who was looking too hard at a 5-and-4 pitcher, a man whose three-year record stood at nine wins and ten losses? In 1957, Koufax walked 51 men, fewer than 4½ men per game. He gave up 83 hits.

His earned-run average was a neat, but not glamorous, 3.89. So who noticed?

Yet there it was. You could gloss over everything else, but you couldn't gloss over that strikeout performance. And to those who did notice, to those few fans who somehow manage to seat themselves at the beginnings of careers, a sense of excitement began to steal over any game Koufax entered. You—if you were one of the few—started to edge forward in your seat when Koufax came on the scene. You waited for the handsome, dark-haired, dark-eyed young man to start popping the catcher's glove. He was starting to get his curve where he wanted it. It wasn't easy. The boy was still more than a touch wild; he often had to come in fat with the 3-and-1 pitch, or the 2-and-0. Batters were timing his fast ball for base hits. Yet the excitement mounted. Always, it seemed, there was a man on base, maybe two, maybe three, and Koufax was straining, taking a huge stride with his right leg and uncoiling the ropelike left arm, throwing his bullets. It was something to look forward to.

Except, of course, there was no more looking forward in Brooklyn. In Los Angeles, the townfolk made ready for Hodges and Furillo and Reese and Campy, and home-raised Duke Snider and Don Drysdale. Sandy Koufax was welcome, of course. But just how did you pronounce that last name?

6

"Like Russian Roulette. With Five Bullets."

LOS ANGELES is a huge city, spreading over 450 square miles. Manhattan Island is all of 22 square miles. Los Angeles has a couple of parks each of which is larger than the principality of Monaco. And it is an odd city, even odder than Brooklyn. People dip their feet or their hands into wet cement outside a movie house in Hollywood. If a kid did this in Brooklyn, he'd get belted by his old man. In Hollywood, the kids who do this are movie actors and actresses, and people applaud.

To this city of the Angels came the Bums from Brooklyn.

Two pieces of property were involved in the Dodger decision to play ball in Los Angeles. One was for a permanent field. The other was a place where the team could play—and make money—until the permanent field was ready.

The two places are the current Dodger Stadium, in Chavez Ravine in Elysian Park. The other is the Los Angeles Memorial Coliseum, where the Dodgers played ball from 1958 through 1961.

First things first. The property at the Coliseum site was

vested in the people of California in 1908, so relates sports writer Paul Zimmerman in his book, *The Los Angeles Dodgers*. An armory, a museum, and other structures were erected, replacing a conglomeration of a race track, barns, saloons, and carnival booths, and the new complex was called Exposition Park. The park stands some few miles due south of the Civic Center, the concentration of downtown government edifices, and borders the campus of the University of Southern California.

In 1921, a stadium was begun that would eventually have a seating capacity of 105,000, a huge saucer rising to dizzying heights from a long grassy ellipse, ideal for football or track or mountain climbing.

But never had it been intended for baseball. Never, until Walter Francis O'Malley viewed those 100,000 seats and saw them as dollar bills.

O'Malley built a diamond pointing roughly northeast, threw up a screen in left field, 250 feet from home plate—the bare minimum allowed under the rules—and permitted his right field to run halfway to Denver.

The field was readied for the 1958 Dodgers. Meanwhile, back at the ravine, other dealings were coming to a head. Chavez Ravine—before the Dodgers—was 300 undulating acres of scrubland, jackrabbits, king snakes, possums, and skunks, plus a handful of ramshackle dwellings, five miles north of Civic Center.

Some people consider the Chavez Ravine conversion to Dodger Stadium a case of give and take. You give. I take.

Los Angeles agreed to cede these 300 acres to the Dodgers. The city agreed to spend up to two million dollars in such improvements as grading and street construction. The Los Angeles County board of supervisors—because some of this was not city property, but county—agreed to provide another $2,740,000 for the building of access roads into the hilly terrain of the park.

In turn, the Dodgers deeded Wrigley Field, an antiquated minor-league ball park, to the city. There was a squabble over mineral rights on Chavez Ravine which became so overwrought most observers gave up trying to follow the proceedings. For a while it appeared that not only was O'Malley ceded land for a ball park, but he had also inviolable rights, in perpetuity, to drill for oil at second base during the off season, or if the Dodgers were losing. Not so. The city retained half the mineral rights. So you see, it wasn't a total giveaway.

The Dodgers built a stadium, at Chavez Ravine, seating some 55,000 fans, and during the building, played at the Coliseum.

In 1958, over 1,845,000 persons saw the Dodgers at the Coliseum, breaking the all-time Dodger record set back in 1947 when the Brooks were winning a pennant. In 1958, the Dodgers didn't finish first. They barely finished. Seventh, to be exact.

Not a moment too soon had the Dodgers fled Brooklyn. It wasn't the neighborhood that was crumbling. It was the team. The slow encroachment of age became swift and

deadly. Baseball careers fell apart before fans' horrified eyes. One career fell apart more tragically before ever reaching the Coliseum. Roy Campanella, finest catcher since Mickey Cochrane, suffered a near-fatal paralyzing spinal injury in an automobile accident.

Don Zimmer, John Podres, and Duke Snider were also banged up in pre-season auto mishaps. In an exhibition game, Zimmer hurt his forehead, chin, and left wrist diving for a ball. Later, he suffered five more injuries in regular play.

Mired down with the Dodgers, and hurting, was Sandy Koufax. Koufax was starting his fourth full season with the club. In the natural order of events, one would expect a definite flowering along about this fourth year, or else a prognosis that no such flowering would ever occur.

The natural order had been tampered with. When the 1957 season ended, Sandy Koufax served a stint in the armed services. A good piece of Koufax's spring training was lost while he fulfilled his obligation to this nation. To some players, this is not a serious loss. To Koufax, it is. Koufax is a slow starter, or, at least, he used to be a slow starter. He seldom won games in April. Each spring, at Vero Beach, he would suffer more than the usual twinges of men whose muscles had gone flabby during the winter. Koufax is invariably afflicted with arm trouble. He is a man of heavy back and shoulder muscles. They tend to tighten up unless he continually exercises them. Today, between innings of a game he is pitching, Koufax may be seen dan-

gling monkey-fashion from the dugout roof as he stretches his arm, shoulder, and back muscles. On the mound, between pitches, he will take time to writhe and twist in an awkward version of a belly dancer.

Koufax was placed on terminal leave from the army on March 4, 1958. Two days later, he joined the Dodgers at Vero Beach. A week-plus, behind schedule. Sandy never really made it up.

Still, he managed to get in shape, and in June of 1958, began to win games as though he had actually entered that flowering phase.

By July 5, 1958, Sandy had won four straight, and his record was a nifty 7-and-3. Then, in the second inning of a game with the Cubs, Sandy collided with Chicago's Jim Bolger while trying to field Bolger's bunt. Koufax suffered a severe spike wound and a badly sprained right ankle. He was on crutches the next day.

When Sandy returned to action, he was plagued by two problems. Rusty, he no longer could find home plate. When he pitched batting practice—so a fellow Dodger said—it was "like playing Russian roulette. With five bullets. You didn't have a chance."

In 1958, Koufax uncorked 17 wild pitches. It is a club record. He walked 105 men, only three fewer than his three-year total up until 1958.

On top of it, Koufax began to experience a new pain. This one was located high up on his back, near his left shoulder blade. The pain, dull at first, became more severe as the 1958 season progressed.

With the injuries and the periods of inactivity, it becomes not too bad a season for Sandy. He finished with eleven wins, eleven losses, far and away his biggest victory season to date. It means, however, that from the time he was spiked, his record was four wins, eight losses the rest of the way.

But when he was hale, Sandy found himself more or less a regular Dodger starter. He started 26 games in 1958, twice as many as he had started the prior year. Aching back and all, he threw 159 innings. He whiffed 131 men in those 159 innings; not his 1 man per inning, but not far back.

There is no doubt Koufax—as most other pitchers—was badly affected by the Coliseum's left field fence, and the net that sat atop the 250-foot marker. Opposing teams stacked their lineups with right-handed hitters, all pulling for the screen. With the exception of John Podres, who managed to adapt himself beautifully both to the physical consequences of the left field nearness and to the psychological barrier that apparently unnerved most pitchers, all Dodger hurlers were constantly taking swift jittery glances at the inviting target. The screen breathed hotly on the backs of pitchers all through the Coliseum's bizarre history as a ball field, but never so much as that first year. For one thing, it was new. For another, the right field wall—so far away it could not be reached by a three wood—was moved in after the 1958 season, and some of the pressure was removed as batters now took an occasional potshot to right.

The Coliseum was a monster that year, and not just to the pitchers. It even managed to tweak both Duke Snider's

strong right arm and his hefty wallet. One evening during pre-game practice, Snider, Don Zimmer, and Ed Roebuck got into a friendly discussion as to whether it was possible to hit or throw a ball over the top of the saucer and out of the park.

Snider elected to throw; Zimmer and Roebuck used fungo bats. Nobody succeeded. Snider lamed his arm, and the Dodgers reprimanded and fined all three, Snider to the tune of $275.

That the public was not satisfied with the Dodgers was made manifest on June 3, 1958. Los Angeles voters went to the polls, to decide—among other matters—whether to approve the city's contract with the ball club for future use of Chavez Ravine. In a surprisingly close ballot, the Chavez Ravine ordinance was barely approved, 351,683 Yes to 325,878 No. Over 48 percent of the electorate had voted against the Dodgers.

Still, Chavez Ravine had passed one obstacle. The Dodgers played out the string in 1958. Tomorrow would be another day. Wait till next year was a cry the Dodgers knew full well. Wait until 1959.

When the 1958 season was over, it was discovered that the reason Sandy Koufax had been suffering pains on the left side of his back was that he had a tumor on his ribs.

7

"That's Nothing. I Usually Cry."

TODAY THERE IS a neat scar high up on Sandy Koufax's back, on the left side. Doctors went in there following the 1958 season, and removed a nonmalignant tumor that had adhered to Koufax's ribs.

Sandy Koufax is apparently doomed to be beset by physical woes all his pitching career. Perhaps all his life. In the glorious year of 1963—following the left index finger problem—Koufax announced rosily his finger felt fine. It couldn't be better. Everybody relaxed. Then Koufax revealed he had a terrific pain in his left shoulder.

Injuries have plagued him. It is a ballplayer's lot to subject his body to a fierce pressure-pot where he may be skulled or spiked, where he will suffer Charley horses and sore arms every spring, where tendons, muscles, and ligaments are always undergoing stress. Yet some players, either blessed by a unique constitution or a mass of good fortune, or both, manage to avoid too many trips to the repair pits. Warren Spahn has pitched about 5,000 innings with one sore arm in the batch.

Koufax makes up for this defection from the law of averages.

In 1959, Koufax moved slowly through spring training, not daring to risk injury to his knitting ribs and flesh. In the process he again strained his throwing arm. He recovered, and pitched his first start on April 12. He was kayoed in three innings, leaving with a 3–0 deficit. The Dodgers went on to win, 5–3. Later, from July 11 through August 1, Koufax was sidelined with a stiff shoulder. In between, he felt the usual Koufax twinges. In short, a typical Koufax year, physically.

Early in the season, when Koufax was experiencing more than usual pains, he received a series of injections to deaden the ache and dissolve whatever it was in the arm that caused the discomfort.

A reporter watched him pitch batting practice one day and when it was over, asked Sandy how he felt.

"Good," Koufax said.

"But you were grimacing every time you threw."

"That's nothing," Koufax said easily. "I usually cry."

All this must be entered, when you realize in 1959 Koufax made a checkered leap forward in his development as the game's most overpowering pitcher. It is the year Koufax struck out 16 Phillies, for a night-game record. It is the year Koufax broke this record while striking out 18 Giants, to tie Bob Feller's all-time one-game strikeout record, and break Dizzy Dean's National League mark set in 1933. It is the year Koufax put together a string of three games in which he struck out 13 Phils, 18 Giants, and ten Cubs. Nobody has touched this total of 41 K's in three con-

secutive games. It is another year Koufax struck out more men than he pitched innings.

And yet, it was an odd year. Typically odd, if there is any such beast. With these credentials, Koufax won a meager 8 ball games, lost 6. His earned-run average—down from the prior year's whopping 4.47—was still a high 4.06.

There were moments in 1959 when Sandy Koufax looked to be the greatest pitcher in the game. There were other moments he was, again, horrid.

If 1956 had been a tight pennant race, it was a laugher compared with 1959. No three-team struggle has ever been so tightly contested as this Dodger-Brave-Giant battle of '59. Through July 4, the Braves led, except for a brief period in May when Cincinnati rose up from fifth place, grabbed the lead, and then slowly began to sag back into the second division. The Giants were never far behind—three and a half on May 24 marked the season low—and the Dodgers, though never ahead until the play-off with the Braves, were always close. Nor was it exclusively a three-game fight. As late as June 21, the first four teams were separated by two and a half games, and Cincinnati, in sixth place, trailed by eight.

Still, it was a Dodgerish year. The Dodgers played an exhibition game on May 7, before 93,103 and in a game that meant nothing in the standings, Carl Furillo broke a rib. The same day, Gil Hodges hurt his shoulder. Later, Hodges injured his leg and sat out a month. The Braves had their share of injuries. Bob Buhl, Bill Bruton, Wes Coving-

ton, Johnny Logan, and Ed Mathews were hurt. For the Giants, Jack Sanford broke his hand and was lost for three-plus weeks. Davenport hurt his knee on August 17 and had to miss most of the furious stretch run. Willie Mays broke a finger.

In this hot pennant race, the Dodgers drew the greatest crowds ever to see baseball in America. With ladies' nights and knothole gangs and exhibitions and later a World Series, the Dodgers drew a total of 3,110,983 to see them at the Coliseum that 1959. Of these, and during regular pennant play, an astounding 2,070,720 paid their way into the great bowl.

Before such mobs, the Dodgers played a wildly exciting brand of ball. Lacking the power of the 1955 club, the Dodgers made it up with pitching, defense, speed, and manager Alston's sleight of hand. They became the master of the one-run victory, the late-inning comeback, the extra-inning win. They won at home and they won on the road. They beat the top contenders, and made it hurt when they walloped the Giants nine of eleven in Seal Stadium.

It was an artful, scrappy club. Surely not the most polished, far from the most powerful. They scratched for their runs. And found them. But more, they wouldn't give an inch. They led the league in fielding, made the fewest errors, laid down the most sacrifice bunts, stole the most bases.

In 1959, the sometimes fit, sometimes aching Koufax got into 35 games, started 23, finished 6. In his 153 innings, he gave up 136 hits and 92 bases on balls—down a hair from

the year before, but still too many walks. There were those 173 strikeouts, an average of 10.18 for every nine innings. Teammate Don Drysdale, who led the league with 242 K's, struck out 8.04 men every nine innings.

As usual, Koufax didn't win a game in April. He stumbled along for two months, and then after nine straight kayoes, he pitched and won a five-hitter on June 17, against Milwaukee, going the full nine innings.

Five days later, Sandy Koufax nudged his way into the record book. In a night game in Philadelphia, Koufax gave up ten hits in a 6–2 win. He also struck out 16 men. Nobody had ever struck out that many in a night contest.

It might have been more than 16, except for the way of a Philadelphia fan. At the end of the seventh inning, Koufax had already recorded his 16th K. But as Koufax started his warm-up pitches for the eighth, a ball fan came down from his seat, vaulted the low railing and trotted onto the field, carrying in his hand a whistle.

Koufax stared nervously at the fan, who walked up to Sandy, put the whistle in his mouth, and blew a shrill blast.

The whole incident had been a $200 dare. The whistle-blower won $200 and then donated the money to an orphanage. There is no telling how much Koufax was unnerved by it all. Suffice it to say, he didn't strike out any more Phils that night.

But he appeared to be on his way, at long last. Five days after the 16-strikeout performance, Koufax shut out the Pirates on six hits, beating them 3–0. It was Koufax's third

complete-game victory in eleven days, the Dodgers' sixth straight win, and the team now had edged toward second place.

Then Koufax hurt his shoulder, was forced to sit out twelve games—at least two, and possibly three starts—and the Dodger momentum was stilled briefly.

Koufax's personal momentum took longer to get underway again. Then, on August 24, against the Phils, who were rapidly becoming Koufax's cousins, the talented but erratic left-hander began another streak of three games that would again thrust him into the record book, and into a status reserved only for the true stars of the game.

Koufax fanned 13 Phils, while giving up just four hits, and winning, 8–2.

A week later, he marched out to the mound at the Coliseum, to face the league-leading Giants. If a single game symbolizes Koufax's career and at the same time highlights a season, this night game of August 31, 1959, before a huge and roaring throng at O'Malley's Chinese Theatre, was it.

A few nights before, a tired Giant team had flown out of Philadelphia, beaten twice in a doubleheader but still clutching a slim lead. On August 28, San Jones righted the Giants, blanking the Dodgers, 5–0, fanning eleven. Willie Mays, broken finger and all, hit a single, double, and home run, drove in three, and contributed his usual fielding heroics. There was a day off, and then the next night the Dodgers evened the series, and on August 31, they were at it again, the Giants leading the Dodgers by two. A Giant

victory would send Rigney's club back to San Francisco with a comfortable three-game bulge. Alston called on Koufax.

There have been few more exciting games in the long history of baseball. Against Koufax was pitted Jack Sanford, husky, hard-throwing right-hander, a man also afflicted in those days with control problems, but again a man who refused to play it safe. If Koufax would lean back, two balls and no strikes, and fire in the high hard one without taking a hair off the ball's speed, so too would Sanford flame away. On top of it, Sanford had recently developed an explosive curve ball, a jet affair that broke wickedly down and away from right-handed hitters.

The Giants struck quickly. With two out in the first, Mays, McCovey, and Cepeda doubled, and the Giants had two runs. The Dodgers had to peck away, getting their two runs one at a time, and they needed the breaks of Sanford's explosive curve twice eluding his catcher and moving Dodgers up the bases.

After the first inning, Koufax turned on the gas. When he struck out the side in the fifth, and again in the sixth, he had 11 strikeouts. But 11 in six innings wasn't going to break Dean's record of 17; you must get your 2 every inning. After eight rounds, it was just—just!—15, and everybody in the Coliseum knew Koufax had to fan all three Giants in the ninth to top Dean and match Bob Feller.

He got shortstop Eddie Bressoud on three pitches.

He got little Danny O'Connell on three pitches.

Up came pitcher Sanford. Sanford is a swinger. He gives you nothing, even at the plate. It would be Sanford who would later break up Ralph Terry's no-hit try against the Giants in the final game of the 1962 World Series.

Koufax struck him out on four pitches, and the noise was like thunder in the soft warm Los Angeles night.

In the bottom of the ninth, the score still tied 2–2, the Dodgers got two runners on. Relief pitcher Al Worthington faced Wally Moon. Moon lifted a fly ball toward left field, and over the beckoning screen, and the Dodgers had won a huge game, 5–2.

"Koufax was so fast that night," said John Roseboro, "that the Giants didn't know what they were doing. Trying to get their bats in front to meet the fast ball, they started to swing early. This meant when Sandy came in with the curve, the hitters couldn't hold back."

And Sandy was coming in with the curve that night. Roseboro gave it a description. "It drops like a chair whose legs collapse."

Sandy Koufax was the toast of Los Angeles. The kid with the promise had fulfilled the promise. Here he was in his fifth major-league season, and only twenty-three years old. Handsome, unmarried, intelligent, reserved. A member of a much honored minority group—a Jew—who won the hearts of Jews and gentiles everywhere when he refused to pitch, refused to put on his uniform, on the holy day of Yom Kippur, Day of Atonement. He would win just 8 games that 1959, but had he lost any of the 8, the team

could not have won the pennant. And he had won this heart-stopper against the Giants.

Koufax, in turn, had grown fond of this big friendly sprawling city of informal dress. He hadn't liked the idea of leaving Brooklyn. His roots were there; his family was there. One reason the Koufaxes had agreed to the Dodger bonus offer relayed to them by Al Campanis was that Campanis had pointed out how convenient it would be, playing 77 games in the borough where you lived. Leaving Brooklyn had been a jolt.

Now he had changed. "The first few days out in Los Angeles, I was lost," Koufax said. "But I soon grew to love L. A. It's a casual town, relaxed. I like that. I made up my mind quickly that I would settle there permanently." It became his home. Soon it became his parents' home.

A week after the big win over the Giants, Koufax lost a game to Chicago, 3–0, but struck out ten Cubs. His total of 41 strikeouts in three straight games broke all previous records, just as did his total of 31 in two games.

The strikeout marks cemented Koufax's hold on the city's fandom. He also became hot copy for the city's press. In a 4–4 game late that season, Alston sent in Koufax in the tenth inning, to pitch relief. Koufax pitched about as well as a man can pitch. From the tenth through the twelfth, Koufax faced nine men, retired nine men, struck out five. Then in the Dodger half of the twelfth, with a man on first and one out, Alston lifted Koufax for a pinch hitter.

The crowd booed Alston, and booed again when the

pinch hitter hit into a double play, and unloosed a final derisive hoot when the Dodgers, behind Stan Williams, lost in the thirteenth, 5–2. The writers second-guessed Alston. Alston noted the change, in Koufax, in the press, and the fans:

"The same critics who had said previously I should never crowd my luck with the 'unpredictable' Koufax now blasted me for lifting a 'hot' pitcher."

Yet "unpredictable" remained a good word. If Koufax was having little trouble getting by the Phils in '59, and less with the Pirates and Giants, the Reds and Cards kept racking him up. When it was over, his earned-run average was over four runs, not a statistic to persuade any manager to hand the ball to Koufax and call in his outfielders. Nor were those 92 walks—better than 5 a game—proof positive that the youngster had finally and forever located the strike zone.

When the year was over, and Koufax was able to look back and see past the strikeout nights and the pennant and World Series victories, he said—with only mild criticism in his words—that he felt he'd been ignored by the management in 1959. That he might have made a greater contribution had he been called on more. It has always been Koufax's feeling, and it is a feeling possessed by most big-league pitchers, that wildness is in good part a by-product of not pitching often enough. You hear it all the time: "I can't sit on the bench, or out in the bullpen, for weeks at a

stretch, and then be expected to get a ball over the plate the first time I'm called on."

There is the obvious retort to such a complaint. How can the management call on a man who is not likely to get the ball over? There is just so much time for experimentation, just so many (or few) laughers when a man can be tossed into a game to see what he can do, and to heck with the final score.

But it was a mild complaint on Koufax's part. He knew he had pitched well often, and when he had not pitched well, he and the management both knew that Koufax had suffered more than his share of aches and pains that long hot summer and even fiercer autumn.

Not that anybody had time for such reflections in '59. The Dodgers went up to San Francisco in September, and again the lead was two games. Los Angeles won the first game of a day-nighter, and in the second—Mike McCormick against Don Drysdale—the Giants took a shaky 1–0 lead, and held it into the seventh. Then on a potential double-play ball, Joe Pignatano, Dodger second-string catcher, took out Daryl Spencer, and the ball spun loose onto the grass of Seal Stadium. Before the inning had finally ended, the Dodgers had scored five runs. The next day the Dodgers won again, and the Giants were through. The Dodgers and the Braves ended it, all tied at the finish of the 154-game season, and in two play-off games, the Dodgers took it all.

From seventh place to the pennant, in one year. No team

had ever done it before. But then, no team had ever been the Los Angeles Dodgers, bums and angels mixed.

In the other league, it was the go-go-go Chicago White Sox, and as always, the American Leaguers were favored to win the classic.

They opened in Chicago, and for nine shell-shocked innings, the oddsmakers were right. The light-hitting Sox went bat mad, powered by castoff Ted Kluszewski, and the slick-fielding Dodgers made three errors in one inning. The final score: 11–0.

In such a game, the Dodgers paraded part of their bullpen crew. Amid the carnage was one Sandy Koufax, making his first Series appearance. Not that Koufax was responsible for any of the carnage. As a matter of fact, he and Clem Labine and Johnny Klippstein held the White Sox to a single hit in the last five innings. But before that, starter Roger Craig had given up five hits in two and a third innings, and reliever Clarence Nottingham Churn III (they called him Chuck, so relax) was touched for another five hits in two-thirds of an inning. When Labine came on in the fourth, the score was already 11–0.

Koufax pitched the fifth and sixth innings, retiring all six hitters, striking out one man. And though there wasn't much pressure on Koufax, it helped manager Alston make up his mind to start Sandy when the Series swung back to the Coliseum.

The Dodgers evened the Series the next day when slender Charley Neal belted two home runs and pinch hitter Chuck

Essegian hit another. The teams traveled to Los Angeles where the White Sox split a gut the first time they saw O'Malley's left field screen.

It was, in a sense, a sidesplitting Series. A disgruntled thirty-six-year-old former employee of a television station in Michigan took out the loss of his job on the rest of the area by sabotaging a transmitting tower, and blacking out the first three games. They arrested him in time for the fans to see games four, five, and six, but assuming a geographic loyalty made most of them White Sox fans, the cable was restored too soon.

It was zany on field, as well. Every Dodger win was directly linked with the relief work of a young man nobody had heard of when he joined the club in the first week of July. His name was Larry Sherry. The big hard-throwing right-hander saved the second contest for Podres. He saved the next one for Drysdale. He bailed out Roger Craig, and got credit. And back in Chicago, he came in early when the Sox began to challenge a huge Dodger lead, and again received credit. Four appearances. Two saves. Two wins.

It is not likely you remember too well Sandy Koufax, in such a Series.

Yet Koufax was involved in one of the more exciting World Series games of recent years, one of the best-pitched games. When the Series switched to Los Angeles, Dodger fans came out in unprecedented numbers. Each game set a new attendance record, and when Sandy Koufax took the mound in the fifth game, the Dodgers leading three games

to one, 92,706 joyous Angelenos swarmed into the oddest of all baseball parks, sitting shoulder pressed to shoulder on wooden planks beneath a startling blue sky and a dazzling sun.

Koufax worked seven innings that gorgeous October afternoon. He gave up five hits and struck out six men. But he yielded one run, and that was the day's story. It was about as undramatic a run as had ever been scored in World Series play, almost as unexciting as the run that won the final game of the 1962 World Series for the Yankees. This run also came in as a result of a double play.

In the fourth, with the score 0–0, Jim Landis singled on a 3-and-2 pitch, hitting a Koufax shoulder-high fast ball. Little Nellie Fox hit an inside fast ball through the middle, and Landis raced into third base. Sherman Lollar swung at a Koufax low delivery, and bounced into a double play, Landis scoring. That was all.

Koufax went out for a pinch hitter in the seventh, and Stan Williams finished up. But all the excitement was generated by Dodger hitters, coming up inning after inning, men on base, trying to nudge home the tying run, hoping to ignite a rally of sorts and win the Series without another trip to the Windy City.

Bob Shaw denied them. Shaw pitched grimly that day, and superbly in the pinches. The Dodgers had nine hits and two walks. They left eleven men on the bases.

In the eighth—with Koufax headed for a bitter defeat and a long, warm shower—the Dodgers threw the huge

assemblage into an upheaval of roaring hope. Wally Moon popped a pitch into short center field. Jim Landis came in, paused momentarily in the blinding sunlight, and the ball dropped in for a single. With one out, Gil Hodges also singled up the middle, and when Landis futilely threw to third too late to nip the sliding Moon, Hodges barged into second. The tying run was on third, the lead run on second, with one out.

Manager Alston sent in left-handed hitter Ron Fairly, to bat for Don Demeter. Lopez jerked Shaw and thrust in the veteran left-hander Billy Pierce. This is all in the tradition of left-handed hitters hitting best against right-handed pitchers, and vice versa. The spinning of wheels became more esoteric. Alston replaced Fairly with right-handed Rip Repulski—to go ahead slightly in the Managerial Maneuvering Marathon—but White Sox boss Al Lopez ordered Pierce to walk Repulski. The bases were loaded, and Alston called on Furillo to hit for catcher Roseboro. Lopez countered by yanking Pierce for right-handed Dick Donovan, and that is how it stood, the crowd momentarily hushed and poised on the delicious blade of expectancy.

Donovan got Furillo to pop up for the second out, and then he got Don Zimmer to pop up for the third out, and the inning was over. Soon so too was the game.

Koufax, the loser, was the forgotten man. Yet in two showings, Koufax had pitched a total of nine innings, and given up one run.

Two days later, the Dodgers blasted Early Wynn, and

before 47,653 chagrined fans, the Dodgers became World Champions for the second time in the club's history. Each Dodger, including Sandy Koufax, became richer by $11,-231.18, largest winning share of any World Series up until then.

Former American League pitcher Dizzy Trout summed it up: "I never saw a bunch of mice lick a cat."

The Dodgers were no tiger, but compared to the punchless Sox, they were a good-sized house cat.

8

"Koufax Can't Throw Anything but a High One."

A BOY BECOMES a man in slow, arduous, and invisible steps. In the process, more than a boy's shins are bruised. Inside someplace—in soul or psyche or slowly growing and storing brain—other bruises take their place. If a boy's physical maturity is a fairly steady matter of height, weight and muscular development, his mental and psychological growth is a stuttering affair, a sort of two steps forward, one step back progression. Sometimes, two steps forward, three steps back.

Sandy Koufax does not boast any such maturing in 1960—he insists, instead, the roof caved in on him—but it is likely the year 1960, the start of a fresh decade, signaled a climax in the inner growth of Sandy Koufax.

It marked Koufax's sixth year with the Dodgers. He'd been on three pennant winners. He'd pitched—and well—in a World Series. The record book was starting to be littered with his name. Yet progress had been terribly slow. Some men make it in one huge leap, from unknown to star.

Willie Mays. Babe Ruth. Dizzy Dean. Bob Feller. Mickey Mantle.

Koufax, star as he is, blessed with such inborn talent that none of the above—Mays, Ruth, Dean, Feller, or Mantle—can claim greater inherent ability, has inched his way to the top of stardom's ladder. After five years, he had won 28 games and lost 27. In five years, he'd completed just 15 games.

Yet progress had been made. Each year Koufax struck out more men than he had the year before, with the exception of 1956, when he duplicated his 1955 total. In five years he'd fanned 486 men, nearly a man per inning. He'd overcome countless injuries. As a starting pitcher he was no longer nursed by his manager and fed only into soft assignments. This is progress.

But it isn't progress that is easily seen. With a pennant winner, Koufax had won just eight games. Inside the young man, it would not have been surprising had a worm of resentment been permitted to grow. He became—in the words of teammate Don Zimmer—a silent sufferer. "You could see he couldn't stand it if we made an error behind him. He remained silent, but you could see."

Coach Joe Becker touches on the same theme. He called Sandy "a silent temper case."

Becker saw it as part of a physical condition, rather than stemming from the psyche.

"Sandy has the opposite of a rubber arm," Becker pointed out. "He has a muscular arm that tends to tighten. When it

does, his control suffers." Now the psyche is called on. When Koufax's control suffered—Becker suggested—he grew silently angry, boiling inside, his body tensing. With this tensing, his arm tightened, and his control suffered further, and the young pitcher was locked securely in the center of an endlessly vicious circle.

With the regression, the silent suffering came to a head and erupted in one angry outburst.

The season began for Koufax in usually dreary fashion. In his last outing during the exhibition training period, Koufax pitched on April 9, 1960 in Fresno, against the Giants. San Francisco belted Sandy unmercifully. Five runs poured across the plate in a single inning. Orlando Cepeda and Felipe Alou hit home runs off Koufax.

Still, this was just spring training.

On April 22, Koufax made his first start. The Cardinals knocked him out in the first inning. Stan Musial hit a three-run double. Daryl Spencer hit a home run. The Cards scored five, and went on to win, 11–7.

Once again, Koufax had been battered in April. Once again Alston stretched out the spaces between starts.

Koufax's next start was on Friday, May 6, against the Phils, in Los Angeles.

It was another incredible performance. In nine and two-thirds innings—or until he and the Dodgers ran out of gas—Koufax held the Phils to nine hits. He walked 7 men, but he struck out 15! In the tenth, the Phils scored five times, and Koufax had lost again.

Koufax waited thirteen days for another start. In Cincinnati on May 19, he went the whole way, leading 4–3 going into the ninth. Then with two out, and after he had struck out 10 men, Vada Pinson hit a triple, and two runs scored. Koufax had lost again, 5–4.

Four days later, Koufax was back in there, starting against Pittsburgh in Forbes Field. In the long history of Forbes Field, pitcher's paradise as it may be, there has never been a no-hitter.

You can't get much closer than Koufax did on May 19, 1960.

Opposing pitcher Ben Daniels got the lone hit off Koufax that day, a looping fly ball that dropped in safely. Koufax struck out 10 men. He beat Pittsburgh, 1–0, for his first win.

In his first thirty-eight and two-thirds innings, Koufax had whiffed 43 men. Yet his record was 1-and-3.

Five days later, the pattern became more established. Koufax pitched thirteen innings. He gave up just three hits. He struck out 15 men.

He lost, 4–3. His record was 1-and-4, and Sandy Koufax, who knew he was pitching as well as he had pitched in his career, could not buy a win.

It is natural that he became discouraged. Now his pitching began to suffer. Manager Alston—a patient man—began to express his doubts about Sandy Koufax. In confidential sessions with Bavasi and other front-office personnel, Alston let it be known that he was not sure Koufax would ever settle down and be the pitcher they all knew he

could become. Less confidentially, Alston told reporters: "Koufax can't throw anything but one kind of ball—a high one."

Talk of a trade with the Yankees began to circulate in the press. The Yankees—it was said—were offering catcher Elston Howard for Duke Snider and a left-handed pitcher. Koufax began to sense the club's discontent. The inner jitters began to step up their tempo.

Koufax knew he had to start producing. But once again he was not getting a chance to produce. Recently in *Sports Illustrated,* he recalled his feelings of those tense, discouraging days:

> The trouble was I'd get a chance to pitch, and then I wouldn't get another chance for weeks. There's your control problem. It wasn't the club's fault: they were always fighting for a pennant. They couldn't take a chance with me. And I had a lot of faults. I'd get mad at myself every time I made a mistake, and it seemed like I made a mistake every time I threw a ball. So then I'd try to throw a little harder, and I'd get a little wilder, and then I'd finally get the ball over, and they'd hit it.

Anxiety began to destroy his effectiveness.

> On every pitch I was thinking about a thousand different things. If I didn't do a good job I might not pitch for a month, so I'd be afraid every time I got to a hitter. I'd

say to myself: "If you walk this man you're out of the ball game, so you can't afford to throw him a curve ball." I'd worry about what the manager was thinking, and what the coaches were thinking. Instead of concentrating on the batter, I'd be looking over my shoulder. Every time I would see the slightest flicker of movement in the bullpen, it would make me nervous. I would lose my concentration and just throw the ball.

It remained silent. There were even those who thought Sandy just didn't care. A teammate viewed the silent Koufax this way: "He has a bad competitive spirit. He never had to ride the bush leagues. He doesn't realize what it means to pitch and win in the majors."

He pitched and he lost, in the majors, that 1960. That is, he lost when he pitched, which wasn't often. His record, when it was over, was eight wins, thirteen defeats. It has the sound and look of a pitcher laboring for a sixth-place team, and not laboring too effectively.

But before the season ended, Koufax had finished with the silent suffering that was tearing him apart. During batting practice one evening at the Coliseum, prior to a game with the Giants, Koufax collared general manager Buzzie Bavasi behind the batting cage, and out it spewed.

"I want to pitch and I'm not getting the chance," Koufax raged.

"How can you pitch when you can't get anybody out?" Bavasi countered.

"How can I get anybody out sitting in the dugout and pitching once a month? If Alston isn't going to pitch me, then trade me. I don't want to sit on the bench the rest of my life. *I want to play.*"

By this time the player and his boss were shouting.

Nearby, Willie Mays and Sam Jones eavesdropped. Said Mays to Jones: "Listen to them go. I hope they trade him to us."

It ended quickly. Nobody was hurt. The tension of pitching for a club that is not winning, and not pitching well, will make a man speak out in anger. Bavasi has always been a matchless handler of men. Perhaps he encouraged this verbal jousting. Perhaps he had sensed the inner bitterness developing in his young charge. Perhaps he had supplied the needle to prick the bag of rage.

Bavasi saw to it Alston pitched the young man more often.

When the season was over, Koufax briefly entertained thoughts of quitting. No, that's not quite accurate. He thought about thinking of quitting.

"I was coming pretty close to thinking about quitting," is the way Koufax put it. "I began to think that maybe putting ten years into something else might be better. At the end of ten years I wouldn't be through, I'd just be starting. Quitting seemed like a possibility." The possibility was just that: possible, but not likely. Quitting did not appeal to Sandy Koufax.

"I had an empty feeling I'd be leaving a job undone."

Man's triumph over himself is seldom accompanied by the pealing of bells, the flashing of lights. But there is in this introspection the look of a man who had searched himself, discovered the flaw, and expressed it. *Expressed*—pressed it out. Now there was the empty feeling of a job undone. The void would have to be filled.

The year 1960 was the last and worst of Koufax's losing years. And yet too much can be made of one season, great or terrible. In many ways, the progress Koufax failed to see in 1960 can be uncovered by peeling back those stats. Never before had Koufax pitched as many innings—175. Never before had he struck out so many men—197. His earned-run average was down again, this time to 3.91, the first time in three years that it had dipped below four runs. He walked 100 men, 5 a game, but it had been worse in the past. And with all his fears of being betrayed by his control and then having to come in with a fat pitch, Koufax yielded but 133 hits all season.

He was coming close, this young self-doubting pitcher. Nor did you have to sift through dry figures to sense the progress, to sense his brushing with greatness. There was something about the young man—you couldn't call him a boy anymore, now that he would be twenty-five—that kept suggesting an ability far beyond mere numbers. Buzzie Bavasi, that shrewd handler of men, sensed it. And so did the enemy, back east.

The Yankees' George Weiss, another perceptive judge of talent, wanted Koufax. He was the left-hander the Yankees

sought, in the deal that would have sent Elston Howard to the Dodgers, and Duke Snider and a pitcher to the Yankees. The trade rumors kept alive. Bavasi and Weiss huddled together, the winter of 1960. Names were kicked back and forth. The Yankees wanted a left-handed pitcher. The Dodgers offered up Podres, an established star, the man who'd beaten the Yankees in the '55 World Series. Podres was a tested pro, but still only twenty-eight years old.

But Weiss didn't want Podres. He wanted Sandy Koufax.

Bavasi said No.

A year later, Bavasi confirmed that the deal had been in the works, and he reaffirmed his faith in Koufax.

"We're gambling big on Sandy," Bavasi said to writer Mel Durslag. "We have had at least six opportunities to trade him for first-class talent." Bavasi fingered the Yankee dickering. "George Weiss insisted on Koufax as the key Dodger in a multi-player deal. We said no. We figured if Weiss wanted someone, he must be good."

The Yankees wanted this pitcher who had never proved himself over a season's pull. Five other teams wanted him. Bavasi didn't need Weiss's evaluation. He had made his own. Bavasi is a man who builds teams. He does not shop for them. Oh, there will be some trading, some buying, some selling. But mainly, the Dodgers either spot their talent on college ball fields, or they grow their talent on the farms. Men like Fresco Thompson and Al Campanis see to it the youngsters are well taught, down on the farm. They are ripened, brought up slowly, and slipped into the lineup

after long, careful testing. Koufax was different. A bonus rule obviated such ripening. But it did not stop Bavasi from watching a boy grow into a man.

In 1961, Sandy Koufax became a towering pitcher.

On the morning of March 23, 1961, Sandy Koufax—professional baseball player—flew from Vero Beach, Florida, to Orlando, Florida, 85 miles distant.

With him were other members of the "B" squad of the Los Angeles Dodgers. They were en route to play a game in Orlando with the Minnesota Twins, the old Washington Senators under a new name. Seated next to Koufax was second-string catcher Norm Sherry.

Koufax was to pitch that day, and Sherry to catch. The battery had their heads together, casually running down the pitching plans. The effects of the conversation that ensued are still being felt.

"If you get behind the hitters," Sherry said (and Koufax probably corrected him in his mind automatically: *When* I get behind the hitters), "do me a favor. Try to throw curves."

When players, or coaches, or managers, or anybody spoke to Sandy Koufax about pitching tactics, it always ended up by the discussion of one word: *control*. The catechism Koufax had preached back in 1955 to *Scholastic* sports editor Herman Masin, the one thing he insisted every young pitcher must practice, was—*control*.

Here he was, nearly six years later, still wrestling with the problem.

Sherry touched a nerve.

"My fast ball is my best pitch," Koufax said stiffly. "I've got to go with that when I'm behind the hitters."

"No you don't," Sherry insisted. "When you force your fast ball—that's when you get real wild. Throw the curve. You can get it over."

"I know I can," Koufax said, "but—" But. The fast ball was his only bread-and-butter pitch.

Or was it?

Wasn't it his peaches-and-cream pitch, his dreams-of-glory pitch? Wasn't it the pitch little boys try to ride to fame on? The fast ball had the glamour. It was Walter Johnson's pitch, Dean's, Bob Feller's. But maybe the curve, after all, was his bread-and-butter pitch?

"Try it my way just once," Sherry went on. "The game doesn't count. It's a great spot to try it out."

Koufax shrugged his shoulders. What did he have to lose? A "B" game in Orlando. The "A" squad—the regulars—were playing a game at Vero Beach. Six years, and he was flying with the "B" squad. He had nothing to lose.

Sherry had another point. When Koufax felt he *had* to throw his fast ball in tight spots, would he please try not to force it? Just throw it with his natural smooth delivery? The ball would get up there fast enough, as is. And Koufax agreed, again.

That afternoon at Orlando, Florida, Sandy Koufax pitched seven hitless, runless innings. The Twins—a slugging club—hit just four balls to the outfield. Koufax struck out 8 men in those seven innings. He also walked 5.

At times, the temptation to shake off Sherry must have been great. He would walk a man and get behind the next batter, and still Sherry would waggle his fingers for the curve. Koufax wanted to rear back and blaze in the Big Bertha. Sometimes, when he had Sherry's "permission" to throw a fast ball, he would let 'er rip. And Papa spanked.

"Every time I reared back and threw, Sherry walked out and made me use change-ups and control."

He threw the curve. It didn't always catch the plate, but five walks in a March ball game isn't too bad. Especially for a pitcher tossing out a lifetime of tactics and building a new style. There were games before this game when Koufax would pitch 95 percent fast balls. Always, when he was in trouble, he'd whip in a fast ball. Not so this March day in Orlando.

Koufax left the game after seven innings, and in the ninth, Minnesota exploded for five runs, to beat the "B" Dodgers, 5–4. Koufax's no-hit stint made a very small splash in the Los Angeles press.

But Koufax knew the score.

Early in the game, Koufax loaded the bases on walks with nobody out. Sherry trotted to the mound and said: "Don't worry about it. Just throw easy."

Koufax followed the advice. It was advice he'd heard before—from Joe Becker, for one—but until this moment he had never been truly able to follow it. Always, he had tried to force the fast ball, search for that little extra something big-league pitchers are always mysteriously calling on

when the bags are loaded. He eased off on his delivery, kept going to the curve ball. It worked.

"I'll never forget it," Koufax said. "I got out of the inning without a run being scored. Then and there I realized that there's no need to throw as hard as I can. In the past I'd go out, and every pitch I threw, I'd try to throw harder than the last one. Now I try to throw strikes and make them hit the ball."

The pieces fell together.

"Looking back now," Koufax said later in 1961 to writer Dave Anderson, "that 'B' squad game changed everything. After that, I had better control and I kept it once the season started. This is the first time since I've been with the club that I'm in the regular rotation."

Control. Control had been the demon. Wryly, Koufax had once compared himself with Whitey Ford. "A sharp guy like Whitey Ford throws for the outside corner of the plate. I'm lucky if I can hit the outside half."

Control had plagued Koufax, would still plague him on other days, other nights. But never again so steadily, so insistently, so disastrously.

Perhaps the Los Angeles press did not realize the significance of Koufax's breakthrough. Koufax sensed it. He celebrated that night, and the consequences of the celebration wiped out any remnant of the no-hitter.

Koufax and pitcher Larry Sherry, brother of catcher Norm who had triggered this small revolution in Koufax's pitching style, went out that Thursday evening for a pizza

meal and a movie. They did not get back to the players' barracks at Vero Beach until 1:45 A.M., Friday.

Manager Walt Alston, on a curfew check, was waiting up for them.

The two ballplayers saw the manager. One of them yelled: "Run!"

They fled for their room.

"Wait a minute," Alston shouted. "I want to talk to you."

Larry Sherry, it has been reported, locked the door. The angry Alston, who happens to be one of the strongest men alive, began to pound on the door. In his fury, he broke the World Series ring he was wearing.

The men finally came out.

The next day, Koufax said succinctly to the inquiring press: "We were out. We were late. That's all."

The men received substantial fines. Alston held a squad meeting the next morning—"to raise a little hell."

Koufax has since elaborated to *Sport* magazine writer Steve Gelman.

"You ever been to Vero Beach?"

"No," Gelman said. "But a writer recently told me about it. He said it's unbelievably dead—a movie, a couple of restaurants, women either over forty or under fourteen."

"That's the town," Sandy said. "Ask anyone."

"When you were fined, though, you made some headlines," Gelman said. "It sounded big."

"I went to a movie and I had a pizza," Koufax said. He shrugged his shoulders. "I'd like to know what else anyone could possibly do in Vero Beach."

There is one Dodgerish postscript.

Koufax is said to have asked Alston: "Why did you beat on the door with your fist?"

"Because I wasn't wearing shoes," Alston explained, in pure logic.

The plane-flight conversation, the no-hitter, and the curfew-busting may not be related. But if they are related, as this observer suspects, you have a neatly packaged personal crisis in the life of Sandy Koufax. And not just the life of Sandy Koufax, Strikeout King.

"The whole difference is control," Koufax said, early in 1961. "Not just controlling the ball, but controlling myself, too."

Control is a funny word. On the face of it, Koufax was "controlling" himself in the days of silent suffering. But he wasn't being fair to himself, or to the club, rigidly controlling the inner smoldering that was keeping him continually on edge, a fretting (but silent!) young man who was being nibbled away by a refusal to express himself. Then one day he told his boss what he felt, fought for his rights and his self-esteem. And the next thing he knew, he was able to absorb into his system advice he'd heard long ago but never really could cope with. A man who controls himself not only knows when to be silent, he also knows when to be forthright—outspokenly, bluntly honest. Sandy Koufax had come to terms with himself.

On April 21, 1961, Sandy Koufax defeated Cincinnati, 5–3, hurling a six-hitter and striking out eleven.

It was his first April win in seven seasons.

He was given more and more assignments. Never had he won more than 11 games. Now he was to win 18. Never had he been asked to pitch so often. His prior high had been 175 innings in 1960. Now Koufax threw 256 innings. Only three pitchers, Lou Burdette (272), Spahn (263), and Don Cardwell (259) pitched more innings. Only three men—Joey Jay, Spahn, and Jim O'Toole—won more games. His 3.52 earned-run average was seventh best in the league. It led all other Dodger pitchers. Only Spahn's 21 complete games exceeded Sandy's 15. And if Koufax still had trouble getting the pitch over—his 96 walks was the league's fifth high—nobody was more "unhittable." Koufax yielded 212 hits, for an average of 7.45 hits per nine innings. Nobody was as low. Ray Sadecki and Joey Jay were a half-hit away.

All these statistics are paraded before you because the tendency remains strong to think of Koufax only as a big strikeout man. Big K. And with reason. But in 1961, Sandy Koufax began to blossom out as the complete pitcher.

Still, there is glamour in strikeouts. In 1961, Sandy Koufax did what people had been waiting for him to do ever since that 14-strikeout performance in his second start in the majors back in 1955.

Koufax broke Christy Mathewson's 58-year-old National League record for strikeouts. Back in 1903, Mathewson had whiffed 267 batters. On September 27, Koufax pitched a gorgeous game against the Phils, a three-hitter in which he struck out 7, and the record was his. Ironically, Koufax lost

that day, 2–1, which is another lesson in itself. You can strike out dozens of hitters, but it is the score that counts. Strikeouts have a way of catching headlines and losing the fish. Late in 1961, up in newish Candlestick Park, the Dodgers blew all chances of catching the Reds, dropping a big three-game set to the Giants. Pitching in relief in the game of September 10, Koufax struck out the side in the fifth inning, whiffing Joe Amalfitano, Felipe Alou and Ed Bailey. Unfortunately, between strikeouts, Jim Davenport singled, Mays walked, and Orlando Cepeda hit a two-strike Koufax fast ball 420 feet into the right field seats for a three-run home run.

Which leads to a last statistic for the year of 1961. Sandy Koufax gave up 27 home runs in his 256 innings, better than one a game. Control of the high hard one may have been improved, but it hadn't been perfected.

That year every fan kept his eye on the Giants, Dodgers, Braves, and Pirates, and with nobody watching, the Reds sneaked in and won the pennant. The Dodgers had their excuses, gobs of physical ones. Duke Snider broke an elbow on April 17, and was out for three months. In desperate need of punch, the Dodgers bought Daryl Spencer, who promptly broke a leg. John Podres suffered recurrent backaches and arm trouble, and missed four weeks. (Then John's father died, and the pitcher missed a turn in September.) Willie Davis crashed into a wall in Chicago, and sat out a spell. Charley Neal hurt a leg in April, developed

a virus, and capped the season's indignities with a case of chicken pox.

Larry Sherry sprained an ankle. Norm Sherry suffered a cracked rib in a collision at home.

Other teams have their injuries. The Dodgers, in '61, were the walking, and sitting, wounded.

But the real reason the Dodgers did not win the pennant is that in head-to-head meetings with Cincinnati, and especially in those "crucial" series that come along from mid-year on, the Reds were the better club.

Sandy Koufax pitched well enough at times against Cincinnati, but his overall record is not impressive. The Reds touched him for 4.30 runs per game, as opposed to Sandy's total ERA of 3.53.

On July 7 at the Coliseum, before a huge crowd that sent the Dodgers' attendance over the million mark, Sandy Koufax and young Ken Hunt took the mound in the first game of a doubleheader. Hunt tried to hand the Dodgers the game. He walked the first three men, gave up a pop-fly double and a wild pitch, and before a man was out, the Dodgers led, 3–0. But manager Fred Hutchinson stayed with the youngster, and the Reds nibbled away at Koufax. A three-run home run by Vada Pinson kayoed Sandy in the fourth. The Reds won; they won the nightcap, 4–1, behind Bob Purkey.

The next time Sandy faced the Reds in Los Angeles, on August 15, he suffered one of those ignominies that embarrass a ballplayer once or twice in every career. In the

sixth inning of a tied ball game, Koufax lined a clean "single" to right field, and loped to first base. Frank Robinson charged the "base hit" and fired to first base, in time to nip the lumbering Koufax.

The next inning, a discouraged Koufax threw a home-run ball to Wally Post, and the Dodgers never caught up. Cincinnati swept the series.

Not that it was a one-way street. Koufax had beaten the Reds in April. He beat them, 10–1, at Crosley Field, on July 20, with a strong seven-hitter. And on August 25, after the Dodgers had staggered through a ten-game losing streak, Koufax righted Los Angeles, besting Bob Purkey, with a five-hitter, 7–2. The game was closer than the score. There was a moment strongly reminiscent of other Koufax days. In the fifth inning, Sandy walked the first two men and hit the next batter, to load the bags with nobody out.

The two hitters coming up were Vada Pinson and Frank Robinson.

Manager Alston came out of the Dodger dugout to speak to his young pitcher.

Pinson popped the first pitch to the infield.

Robinson grounded the first pitch on two hops to Maury Wills, and a 6-4-3 double play ended the frame, while on the Red bench, players second-guessed Pinson and Robinson for going after the first pitch with Koufax having control difficulties. Koufax breezed the rest of the way.

Not that Koufax pitched only against the Reds. He had some dandy days against other tough-hitting clubs. One of

them was a classic duel with the Cardinals' strong right-hander, Bob Gibson. On April 25, Koufax edged Gibson, 1–0, tossing a three-hitter. Four days later, Koufax beat the Cards again, this time, 2–1, and again he gave up just three hits. He also struck out 13. He shut out the Cubs, 3–0, on a brilliant two-hitter, while whiffing 14 on June 20. Twelve days later, Sandy was named to the National League All-Star squad.

He deserved the honor. He'd been the first pitcher in the league to win 6 games, the first to win 8, the first to win 10. Just before the All-Star break he was 10-and-3. Sandy tailed off the rest of the way, ending up 18-and-13, but it remains his first fine full season.

Manager Alston disdained credit for the sudden improvement. When it was noted that in the first 150 innings of '61, Koufax had walked only 55 men—far below his usual figure—reporters crowded around Alston to inquire of this abrupt change.

"The credit belongs to him and Joe Becker," Alston said. "They worked on it together. Some people wonder if he's just having a hot streak, but I doubt it. He's been so consistent for so long that I'm sure it's not a hot streak."

Not that it was smooth as satin. Koufax still hadn't absorbed all the learning into his style.

"I still sometimes forget," he said late in 1961. "One night in Milwaukee, the Braves got a couple of runners on and I got mad and tried to throw harder. I was out of the ball game."

There were physical flaws. While pitching against the Phils in a game that season, Koufax unconsciously began to telegraph his pitches. Manager Gene Mauch noted that when Koufax prepared to throw a curve, he invariably held his elbows away from his body. While winding to fire his fast ball, the elbows were tucked in tight. Mauch passed the dope to his coaches and batters.

"The information didn't help much," Mauch related sadly. "When Sandy is having a good day, when he's throwing that 'radio ball,' about all a hitter can do is be grateful Sandy doesn't pitch more often. Koufax has had the best arm in baseball ever since he came up. It was just a question of when he'd learn to pitch."

A "radio ball" is a pitch so fast it is heard, but not seen.

Still, a pitcher who telegraphs his pitches is not going to get away with it very long. Coach Joe Becker became aware of the flaw in Koufax's delivery. Becker is a man who sees the whole picture. He effaced this one hitch, but it was not enough. Becker searched his charge to make sure all was right—elbows, stride, follow-through, timing, the works. For six years he had worked on Koufax to convert the scatter-armed boy into a well-oiled pitching machine. In 1961, he and Koufax saw the light.

"Sandy's shortened his stride on his front foot," Bavasi pointed out, when he too was asked how come Koufax was suddenly getting everybody out. "That helps his control. Batters used to 'read' his pitches. He showed the ball when he brought it up. Now he hides it. He used to get too upset.

He'd hurry. I told him: 'Nothing can start until you get damn good and ready to pitch. Whatever you do, don't rush it.' "

Koufax picked up little self-help habits. It's easy enough to say "don't rush," but Koufax found the counsel difficult to carry out. He'd throw and the catcher would return the ball to him, and in a few seconds, he'd throw again. It was the only thing he could do. It was, in fact, his job. Here's a baseball, and there's the batter, so let's go. But he knew he was rushing the cadence. He explored the problem, and discovered that Pedro Ramos, for one, would spend much time fussing with the rosin bag, to help slow his rhythm. Bob Turley would take several deep breaths. Deep breathing relaxed Turley, and it also passed time. Lou Burdette talked to himself.

So Koufax began to fuss with the rosin bag, take deep breaths, and talk to himself. He stopped hurrying.

Joe Becker saw it as a lesson in relaxing.

"The biggest thing Sandy's done was that he learned to take it easy. You know the expression, 'Reach back and put something extra on the ball'? Well, the expression is all wrong. What matters is what a pitcher does with his hands and wrists in front of his body, not behind him. When he tenses up and tries to throw too hard, that's when he gets in trouble. When he relaxes and throws with a nice, loose wrist, his pitches do things. Koufax just had to learn to relax."

That season, with Koufax winning and setting his strike-

out record, a discussion began that still continues. Just how fast is Koufax? Is he the fastest pitcher ever? How does he compare with Bob Feller?

Joe Becker offered his opinion.

"This season, and before, too, people have compared Sandy's speed with Feller's. But I'd have to say no. Sandy is fast, as fast as anyone in baseball today, but he doesn't have the super speed that Feller had."

But that is the category Koufax was now in.

Mel Durslag tells an anecdote that serves to close down this 1961 season. It may be a mite apocryphal. In September of 1961, Alston unwittingly scheduled Koufax to pitch a ball game on Yom Kippur, probably the most holy day on the Jewish calendar. Koufax asked to be excused. Stan Williams replaced Koufax in the rotation for that day, and was beaten.

Alston was immediately criticized by irate fans for not planning his pitching rotation to make allowance for Jewish holidays. A fan mailed Alston a 1962 calendar, with all the Jewish holidays marked.

"There'll be no slip-ups this time," Alston promised soberly.

There were no slip-ups in 1962.

Just total disaster.

9

"I Feel Like Job."

BACK IN THE 1880's, when baseball did not pay as much as it does today—what does?—a ballplayer named Thomas "Toad" Ramsey used to supplement his pitching income with an off-season bricklaying job.

One day he sliced a tendon in the index finger of his pitching hand and found, when the hand had healed, the tip of his finger stood at a sharp angle to the rest of the finger and would not unbend.

The result was the invention of Toad Ramsey's fingertip —or knuckleball—pitch. The injury proved a blessing. Ramsey could deliver up a ball that had no spin and tended to float or sink in weird, unpredictable patterns. Ramsey mastered the delivery, and in a game in 1887 while pitching for Louisville, struck out 17 Cleveland batters. That year a new rule had been written into the books, allowing a hitter four strikes instead of three. The rule was written out of the books at the season's end. But in between came Ramsey's fingertip 17-strikeout performance, which must rate as one of the masterful pitching jobs in the history of baseball.

Robert Smith in his delightful panoramic *Baseball in America* says of Ramsey: "There were people who said that

he could have struck out everybody if he'd really had a mind to." Unfortunately, he hadn't a mind to. He liked his whisky more than his baseball.

Then there was Mordecai Brown, of the Chicago Cubs. They called him Three-Fingered Brown. For good reason. He had four fingers. Or, four and two-thirds. He had lost part of one finger on his pitching hand, and the affliction gave him such odd stuff nobody could put a bat to it. His duels with Christy Mathewson are legendary, with Brown besting Mathewson in two vital games in the 1908 pennant race, won by the Cubs.

And Sandy Koufax makes three.

There is one small, vital difference. In the case of Sandy Koufax, and the circulatory difficulty that seized his left hand in the middle of the 1962 baseball season, the injury did in no way make a better pitcher of him. It almost destroyed his career.

It also helped establish a yardstick by which Sandy Koufax may be measured. Not simply a measure of pitching under duress. Nor one of courage. He proved his courage, he proved his ability to perform under adverse conditions. The yardstick we are talking about is a more primitive measure. It stacks a Sandy Koufax, one finger made useless, the pain of pitching made nearly intolerable, half his arsenal (the curve ball) nullified, against the National League's healthy, strong, talented pitchers.

The comparison could be made most sharply in a ball game played in San Francisco on July 8, 1962. The index

finger of Koufax's left hand was numb that day. He could not spin off a curve. He threw fast balls at the Giant hitters, a murderous crew of sluggers who could drive baseballs through the San Francisco wind at Candlestick Park and over the distant fences, or who would cleverly ride the wind to right field, and let the ball soar out of sight.

In the Giant dugout, the never-still Al Dark began to notice a pattern to Koufax's pitches that Sunday afternoon. Fast ball. Fast ball. Fast ball. Nothing but. Yes, one change-up. Everything else fast balls. Along about the third inning, Dark went down to the dugout. He said to each hitter: "He's not going to give you anything but fast balls today. Be ready." The Giants nodded. The pennant race was impossibly tight. Whoever won the day's ball game would be in first place.

Against Koufax was Billy O'Dell, having his finest season. O'Dell is an enormously talented pitcher, a left-hander with a strong fast ball, a good curve, superb control, great courage, and undiminishing stamina. That day he had all his stuff.

But going into the ninth inning, the Dodgers led, 2–0. For five innings, Koufax had a perfect game. He began to tire, finally, before the crushing pressure of going to war with but one weapon, and that one exactly the kind of weapon a great hitting team relishes in a pitcher. If a batter is dead sure all he is going to see is fast balls, he licks his lips and digs in, and the result is usually a barrage of baseballs, filling the distant sky.

Not so this July 8. Koufax had just his fast ball. His fast ball and a numb index finger. But the Giants were helpless for eight-plus innings.

In the ninth, Koufax had to come out, after a base hit and a walk, but Dodger relief pitching preserved the win and the shutout.

It was Koufax's thirteenth win. His strikeouts zoomed over the 200 figure. The Dodgers moved into first place. They stayed there, alone, until the last day of the season.

Koufax had provided the yardstick. Half a pitcher that day, he was better than one of the best in the league.

Nine days later, doctors were wondering whether Koufax's finger would have to be amputated.

In 1962, the Dodgers moved out of the Coliseum. For good. The Coliseum had served nobly, if at times ludicrously. Now it could be returned to the Rams and other beasts. The Dodgers would play in a stadium in Chavez Ravine. Today this is what most fans call the stadium—Chavez Ravine. Walter O'Malley calls it Dodger Stadium. The result has been that the stadium has two names, if for no other reason than that the Los Angeles Angels, of the American League, also play there. The Angels pay rent to Mr. O'Malley. They refuse to pay him and his team homage. To the Angels, the field is Chavez Ravine. This, too, is Los Angeles.

Dodger Stadium, or Chavez Ravine, it is a magnificent baseball park, perhaps the most beautiful ever built. The

decks of the stadium rise in pastel-painted tiers; the remotest seat commands a startling view of the proceedings below. Beyond the distant bleachers and pavilion sections of the outfield are brown hills. At night, a city of lights twinkles on the horizon.

The Dodgers—bless their publicity-seeking hearts!—announced at first that Dodger Stadium was provided with as much lighting power as the entire city of Seattle. After the first night game, where fans stared at the well-lit field—but no better than well-lit—Angelenos began to send books in Braille up to Seattle.

But it was beautiful, and is. Even hardened easterners, weaned on a derogation of all things Angelic, are awed by their first sight of the stadium. In contrast, Candlestick Park has an unfinished quality to it, a stone-cold look that neutralizes the emotions. O'Malley's great pasture is warmly alive, bright and friendly.

Which is not to say the field and stadium are perfect. For the first months of the 1962 season, it was feared some spectator would succumb to thirst. No one could find a drinking fountain. There was plentiful other liquid, and a cynic might have been heard to suggest that O'Malley had taken a leaf from Marie Antoinette. "Let 'em drink beer!" could have been the cry of 1962.

Moving from one tier of the stadium to another was nearly impossible. There were stairs, but the doors to the stairs were usually locked. There was an elevator, but one elevator and thirty or forty thousand people—Well, you can imagine.

The surface of the field was baked hard by southern California sun. The Dodgers liked it this way. A water-softened infield meant infielders could get to ground balls and throw out runners. The Dodgers were a running team, not a slugging team. The field stayed rock hard.

But with these flaws, it remained a marvelous playing field. Mineral rights or not, O'Malley had magnificently performed his share of the contractual obligation.

For half a season that 1962, so had the Dodgers. For half a season, so did Sandy Koufax fulfill his role.

In past years, National League pennant races have thrilled ball fans all over the nation. In nearly every dogfight season, the Dodgers have been in the thick of things.

Never more so than in 1962.

Excitement is bred into Dodger ballplayers. The 1962 squad bristled with excitement. They ran with blinding speed; they stole bases with brazen disdain; they became experts at milking runs from the opposition, at hoarding slim leads. You seldom saw a Dodger game in which either the Dodgers or their foe leaped off to a big lead and held it without real challenge. You sweated for runs; when you lost, it was always bitter, always tense. You can run your finger up and down the Dodger roster—exclusive of pitching—and the question isn't: How come they lost? It is: How come they nearly won?

There are no superstars, of the Mays, Aaron, Frank Robinson ilk. For all its speed and its ability to con the opposition out of runs, it is not a lineup to frighten other teams.

The answer is pitching.

For half a season, it appeared that Sandy Koufax would have the finest year any pitcher has had since Dizzy Dean won 30 games in 1934. Koufax had won 18 games the year before; this time he would win 13 by the All-Star break and one immediately after the break. He had lost 4. After 88 team games, he had struck out over 200 men. Not only was his own National League record of 269 strikeouts within easy reach, not only was Bob Feller's modern mark of 348 strikeouts in 1948 within not-difficult reach, but there was a flitting chance Koufax might go on to fan 400 hitters. The pitcher's Mount Everest.

He was practically unbeatable, for half a year.

On April 10, before an opening-day crowd of 52,564 in new Dodger Stadium, Wally Post drilled a long home run over the left center field fence, and Cincinnati had beaten the Dodgers, 6–3. The next day, Sandy Koufax evened the series, and the season, with a four-hitter. Koufax won a second game that April, the first time he had ever won two ball games so early in any season. Then he won a third and a fourth, all in April.

One of them was a big one. This is a nation of cynics. We praise our heroes, and then add the word BUT. Back in 1959, Koufax had struck out 18 Giants in a night game at the Coliseum. You remember the cynics, that night. The Los Angeles Coliseum was literally the city of the blind. Call those lights? Chimneys are better illuminated. He struck out 18? Why so few.

On April 24, in Chicago's Wrigley Field, where all games

are played by day, Koufax whiffed 18 Cubs, in a six-hit, 10–2 win. He said later the performance pleased him more than any other pitching feat of the past.

Now he stood alone in the record book. Bob Feller had struck out 18 men just once.

Koufax slumped briefly in May, and then picked up again, whipping the Giants, 8–1, on May 21, while fanning ten. The pennant had become a horse race. The Giants had gone off on a 10-game winning streak at the end of April, and talk about pitching, the Giant pitchers—Marichal, Sanford, Pierce, and O'Dell—put together 7 complete games in a row. By May 1, the Dodgers had fallen to fourth place, but their record was a solid 14-and-8, and they were only 2½ games behind the flying Giants. By the middle of May, the Giant lead was sliced to a game, and the Dodgers were second.

Koufax kept winning, and the Dodgers kept winning, and early in June, Los Angeles displaced San Francisco. The Dodgers won 13 in a row, to tie a 1953 club record, but never would they be able to open up a comfortable distance between themselves and the hated Giants.

The Dodgers got a break, of sorts, but they were going to need some luck. In the off-season, the Giants had purchased Billy Pierce from the American League, and the wily left-hander started an incredible winning streak in Candlestick Park that would last all year. But on June 14, Pierce was spiked in Cincinnati, and lost for nearly four weeks. The Giants absorbed the blow and fought doggedly.

Still, with Koufax having the year of his life, the year of

any pitcher's life, and with Don Drysdale the towering pitcher *his* potential always had suggested, and with such as John Podres and Stan Williams winning as starters, and Ed Roebuck winning in relief, and young Ron Perranoski saving game after game, it appeared that the Dodger pitching depth would be enough to sustain the club in face of Giant power.

But our story is Koufax. He struck out 10 Giants. He struck out 16 Phils. He struck out 13 more Phils, and it was June 13, 1962, and he was just warming up. In his next eight starts, through July 12, Sandy Koufax yielded a total of four earned runs. On the day the streak began—June 13—he hit a home run, first of his career, to beat the Braves, 2–1, on a three-hitter.

He hit the home run off Warren Spahn.

The statisticians were now thumbing the record books. In June it was revealed that this one-time erratic thrower had amassed the lowest walk record per inning of any 1962 Dodger.

On June 18, he hooked up in a pitching duel with Bob Gibson of St. Louis that the batters—as they say—played by ear. Fast balls buzzed through the night like bullets. Gibson is a big husky right-hander, a magnificent athlete, poised and strong, a man who hits baseballs out of sight, runs well, and fields his position like a shortstop. Koufax is—well, Koufax. When his fast ball is humming, as it hummed that night and all that first half-season, you might as well wear a blindfold for all the good looking will do you.

In the ninth inning of a 0–0 game, Tommy Davis belted a Gibson fast ball over the wall, and the Dodgers had won, 1–0. Koufax struck out 9.

Most significantly, in this terribly tense ball game against a hitting club almost as powerful as the Giants, Koufax did not walk a single man. It was a first. Never before had he started and finished a ball game without a walk.

Walter O'Malley had a comment. "Sandy came from the cradle to the major leagues. He never had any minor-league experience. The boy is just now learning the game."

He was learning the game. And it wasn't just a game. Back in 1955, he had told Herman Masin the game wasn't peaches and cream. But he really didn't know. Now he was in his eighth year. The league had grown to ten teams, and with the growth, the travel situation had become more wearing. Early in 1962, Koufax said: "All this travel, it's crazy, man. I don't know who thought up this schedule, but whoever it was, he should be made to travel through it."

The Dodgers had opened at home in 1962, flown up to San Francisco for two games, flown to Cincinnati for two night games, got a day off, and then were in Milwaukee for three games, the last one at night. The next afternoon they were playing in Chicago. In another wearying stretch during the end of May and beginning of June, the team played 14 games on 12 consecutive dates, and in so doing traveled from New York to Philadelphia to Pittsburgh to Houston.

It wears out a man. Even a six-foot-two-inch, 200-plus-pounder.

But perhaps what Koufax was saying when he complained briefly about the schedule complexities was something far removed from the surface.

His finger had begun to bother him.

"I first began to notice something in May," Koufax later told Robert Creamer, of *Sports Illustrated*. "My finger would feel sort of numb. It didn't hurt, and it didn't bother my pitching, but it was numb. Then—I guess in June—it would go white, sort of a dead white. No color in it at all. If I pressed my thumbnail against the finger and made a depression in it, the depression wouldn't come back up."

Sandy Koufax never has said so, but it would appear he was frightened by the condition of his finger, back in May of 1962.

Exactly what was happening to Koufax will probably never be fully learned. The words the doctors have given the condition tend more to name it than to explain it. It was—as a doctor said—"a circulatory malfunction adversely affecting the left index finger." It was, as a doctor said, "a vascular ailment resulting in an arterial blockage."

But why the malfunction of the circulatory system? Why the arterial blockage? What caused it?

A cardiovascular specialist, Dr. Travis Winser, thought the blockage originated in Koufax's left shoulder and suggested that Sandy undergo an operation. Koufax declined.

It was thought that the bunched muscles of Koufax's heavy shoulders and back had caused an artery to be pinched shut, or nearly shut. There were other possibilities.

The diagnosis at last seemed to settle on a blood clot in Koufax's left hand. But all agreed: the blood to Koufax's left index finger was being cut off. When any tissue of the body is not sufficiently washed with blood—carrier of precious oxygen—the tissue slowly atrophies and dies.

As Sandy Koufax worked his way through May and into June, and through June—winning and pitching as no pitcher of recent time—the left index finger was unmistakably starting to die.

Sandy Koufax is a loner. He is a bachelor. He lives by himself. Ballplayers respect him, but they tend to be put off somewhat by his studious ways. Koufax reads. He listens to fine music (just as he listens to not-so-fine music). He is intelligent, sensitive, introspective. He keeps to himself.

Another man, early in May, the finger going numb, might have gone to either of the two Dodger trainers, Bill Buhler, or Wayne Anderson, or to either of the two club physicians, Dr. Robert Woods or Dr. Robert Kerlan. He might have gone directly to Buzzie Bavasi and said: "Look at the darn thing. It's numb."

Instead, when he was alone he would press his thumbnail against the fingertip and watch with curiosity as the half-moon depression didn't bounce back up, the way it did on the other hand.

June began to fade, and the race heated up with the weather. On June 20, the attendance at Dodger Stadium went over 1,000,000. It was only the thirty-third home game. The Giants won five in a row, and on June 26, re-

gained the lead. Two days later, the Dodgers were back on top. The next day it was the Giants, and on June 30, 1962, the Dodgers were at home to play the Mets, with Sandy Koufax the pitcher.

You know about the game. This was Koufax's first no-hitter. But now it is in context. He pitched this superb game with a dangerously sick finger on his throwing hand.

It was not really much of a game. In the bottom of the first inning, after Wills and Gilliam had gone out, the Dodgers scored four runs on five hits and a base on balls. The Met pitcher was Bob Miller. He hadn't won a game all year. Ray Daviault replaced Miller after the damage had been done, and pitched tight ball the rest of the way. In the seventh inning, with two strikes, Frank Howard swung with one hand and drove a gigantic fly ball over the fence for a home run. In the bottom of the eighth, just to remind the fans that the home run was not the usual Dodger weapon, Maury Wills stole second and then third—with a 5–0 lead!—and the crowd settled back for the top of the ninth and the Mets' last chance to touch up Koufax.

Over at third base, in the coaching box, Solly Hemus had kept up a running chatter all night long, directed at Koufax and his growing no-hitter. "You've still got that no-hitter going," Hemus would chirp, hoping to rattle Koufax, hoping to cash in on the old myth that one must never mention an incipient no-hitter for fear of jinxing it.

"I knew I had a no-hitter going, too," Koufax said bluntly.

He is not stupid. He had a no-hitter going, and he pitched

for it. His fast ball was a blur and despite the numb fingertip he was breaking off huge curves. He put the change-up in moth balls. The change-up is a lovely pitch, baffling to the hitter, and bewitching to the viewer. But if it floats up high and a batter takes his time, it becomes a vulnerable pitch.

There is more. A man goes to war, he takes his big guns. The caveman didn't throw mudballs. He threw rocks. The tension of this no-hitter made it a war. Met coach Hemus made it a war. Knowledge of what was transpiring made it a war. Koufax threw his big guns into the war: the fast ball, the curve.

"I wasn't going to risk anybody getting a hit off the change-up," he said.

It was more than risk. It would have been bitterly frustrating to blow down 26 batters with the heavy artillery, and toss up a mudball to the 27th and see it popped over the shortstop's head, to fall in on the grass, or topped slowly down the third-base line, beaten out for a base hit.

In the ninth inning, the first listed batter was pitcher Daviault. On the Met bench were right-handed Gil Hodges and Charley Neal. The inherent drama of calling on an ex-Dodger to attempt to spoil a Dodger no-hitter was not lost on the audience. Spectators craned their necks. Who would it be—big Hodges or spidery Neal?

Out of the dugout strode Gene Woodling. The next day Casey Stengel was astonished at the Los Angeles fans. "Didn't they ever hear of Woodling?" he asked.

They had heard of Woodling. They expected a right-

handed hitter. Woodling hits left. Woodling was for years a hitting machine, a man who tattooed line drives to all fields, a man who hit with occasional power, but who nearly always got a piece of the ball. He was not a wild man at the plate. He waited for his pitch. He refused to fish. Now he was aging, as players go, but he was not through. He would hit .274 for the Mets that season.

Koufax bent over a strike. Then his control lapsed. This was not the sharpest performance of Koufax's life, for all the overpowering quality. He was a mite wild. Four times in a row he missed to Woodling, and the Mets had their fifth base runner. To reduce the possibility of the double play, Stengel replaced Woodling with young Joe Christopher. Double plays had wiped out two of the prior walks.

Richie Ashburn was the next batter. It had been Ashburn who had given the game its immediate tip-off, the first batter in the first inning. Koufax had blown him down with three pitches—Ashburn, who struck out as seldom as any man in the league.

In the sixth, Ashburn had also given the crowd a moment of jitters. His slicing line drive had been lost in the lights by Tommy Davis. Then Davis recovered for the catch.

Now Koufax whipped in a strike. A fast ball was inside, to even the count, and then in came another fast ball on the outside corner. Ashburn punched at the pitch, and a line drive went ripping into left field, curving. The drive landed some 15 feet foul. With the count 1-and-2, Ashburn topped a ground ball to Wills, who tossed to Larry Burright for the

force on Joe Christopher. Ashburn beat the relay to first. There was one out.

Now it was Rod Kanehl, the versatile Met. Kanehl had struck out in the first and the fourth. In the seventh he had grounded to short.

On Koufax's first pitch, Kanehl hit a ground ball to third where Jim Gilliam gobbled it up and fired to Burright—for the second out—and again Burright's return to first failed to conclude the double play.

The last man. Felix Mantilla. Mantilla had struck out in the first (every Met had struck out, except Frank Thomas), had bounced into a double play in the fourth, and walked in the seventh.

Koufax curved him high, for a ball. A fast ball missed—low—for ball two. Mantilla popped a fast ball foul, back to the screen. And on the next pitch, Mantilla hit a high bounder to shortstop, where Maury Wills grabbed it and threw to Burright for the final out.

The no-hitter was in the books.

The next day, this observer was in the Dodger clubhouse, visiting with Tommy Davis, for a magazine article. Sandy Koufax came in early, and accepted congratulations. He signed some score cards of last night's game, and he spoke briefly about the game, comparing it in thrills with his 18-strikeout days. But there was more than a sense of reserve about Koufax that day, more than his natural reticence. He seemed more than just weary. He seemed burdened.

Nobody knew it, but his finger was worse. Before, it had

not hurt, it had just felt numb. "It had no color, no life," Koufax had said. He said he hadn't been unduly troubled by it. "I wasn't worried too much," he recalled, in retrospect, but the words are interesting. Not worried *too* much. Just a little. Why else the ritual of digging the thumbnail into the fingertip, to see whether it had any feeling, any life?

In his next appearance, the finger began to affect Koufax's ability to throw a curve. Yet he beat the Phils, 16–1, on July 4, on a five-hitter. He struck out 10. In his last three shots against the Phils, Koufax had struck out 39 batters, an average of 13 per game.

July 4 is the traditional halfway mark in baseball. The team that leads on July 4 is usually considered the favorite to win the pennant. On July 4, after Koufax's victory, the Dodgers led the Giants by half a game.

But with all these joyous statistics, one fact loomed grimly large. Koufax was not able to throw his curve. "I couldn't spin the ball off my fingertips."

The Dodgers headed for San Francisco, for a three-game meeting with the Giants. On July 8, Koufax beat O'Dell and the Giants, throwing nothing but fast balls. The next day the Giants threw the Dodgers a curve—of sorts. The management ordered the infield watered heavily before the game, and the Dodgers were hobbled by the near-mud. The Giants won the final two games, and led once again.

Four days later, Koufax started to reach the end of the line for 1962. Once again it was the Mets, and once again Koufax appeared to be a superb pitcher. But a one-sided

pitcher. The numbness was wearing off. Pain had started to set in. He pitched seven innings, and went out leading, 3–0. Larry Sherry completed the shutout, and Sandy had his 14th victory.

It was to be his last.

Now he was talking about the difficulty. He had to talk about it, because the distress was so evident. Circulation to the index finger had all but stopped. Circulation to his thumb and middle finger was partially limited.

Koufax made one more start that July. On the 17th he lasted one inning in Cincinnati before coming out. The Reds battered him for three hits and two runs. A blood blister had formed on the tip of Koufax's index finger. Pitching with an unnatural motion, in an attempt to relieve the distress to his finger, he developed an ache in his shoulder.

He flew home to Los Angeles on Wednesday morning, July 18. Doctors examined the sore hand, and finally decided that a blood clot had probably formed in the meaty part of the hand where the thumb, index finger, and palm come together. Doctors speculated that the clot—if indeed it was a clot—had probably been caused by a trauma of some sort, a blow. They asked Koufax whether he had been hit on the palm.

Koufax knitted his brow. In 1963, he was to recreate his thoughts. "I think I know when it happened. I throw left-handed, but I bat right-handed. Early last season I decided to bat lefty, because that way my right arm would be nearer

to the pitcher than my left, and if I was going to get hit by a pitch I'd rather have it hit my right arm than my left. So I batted left and I got jammed by a pitch on my hands, and I think that's when the trouble started."

No one will know for sure. It might have been a fast ball inches above Koufax's fists as they were curled about a bat handle. Batting left, his left hand was higher and nearer to a baseball that rattled against his bat and jolted his palms. The irony of Koufax batting left-handed to protect himself, and nearly destroying his career, is sharp indeed.

Whatever the cause, doctors soon had an exotic name for Koufax's condition. They called it the Reynaud Phenomenon, after a Frenchman with a penchant for soccer. In lay terms it meant a circulation disorder, the blood pinched off because of some blockage, such as a nearby clot.

For all its exotic nature, it has not been totally uncommon among pitchers. Or some version of it. Jack Sanford has had circulation difficulty in his right index finger and other parts of his hand for years. Sanford would rub the hand vigorously with rosin to restore circulation. Other pitchers have observed the same odd loss of sensation.

But Koufax's was by far the worst on record.

The first reports out of the Los Angeles medical consultations were that Koufax would be lost for at least two weeks. This would mean three or four starts. The doctors had prescribed anticoagulants to dissolve the clot. But the condition proved more stubborn. Koufax had let it go too long. Doctors measured the circulation in Koufax's index finger at

15 percent. Normal runs around 85 percent. Just a tiny dribble of blood was reaching the fingertip. With the treatment came intense pain.

"This is intolerable," Koufax said. "I can't touch anything. It's like touching fire."

The finger began to look awful. The blister at its tip broke. The skin began to flake off. It became obvious that the first reports were overly optimistic. Not two weeks. Not four weeks, as the second estimates had it. Six weeks, two months for sure.

Actually, the doctors were soothing Koufax's worries. They knew something he didn't know, and they wanted to see which way events would go before any dire news would be released. Perhaps it would not have to be released. That is what they were fighting for. The question before the doctors was not when would Koufax be ready to wrap his big left hand around a baseball and propel it past National League hitters. The question was whether it would be necessary to amputate the finger.

The doctors knew that a 15-percent circulation was not enough to sustain the finger. More than a dribble of blood was needed. The anticoagulants had to work, or else the finger would have to go.

The drugs began to take hold. Koufax was ordered to rest, to give the medicine every chance to attack the blockage to the precious digit. And when the circulation began to increase, as it finally did begin, the unaccustomed flow of blood intensified the already severe pain. The finger was

raw and ripped—"like a piece of raw meat," Koufax has described it—and the tip began to blacken.

"I feel like Job," Koufax said, buttressing himself against the discomfort, with the leaven of dry humor. "I can't get mad at anybody except the Lord, and if I do that, I'm afraid things will get worse."

To the Dodgers, the blow was a Job-like stroke of fate. It is to the team's everlasting honor that when a disabled Koufax left the squad, the Dodgers went on to win 17 of their next 21 games. If nervous flutters seized the club in the last ten days of the campaign when an overworked pitching staff wore out and the hitters stopped hitting, it must be recalled that the immediate reaction to the loss of the league's finest pitcher was not of defeat or of despair. The players dug in, dedicated themselves to the task ahead, and for nearly a month performed sheer heroics, day after day.

The team brought up young Pete Richert, a left-hander with a blazing fast ball, but erratic. A young Koufax, they said. Richert did what he could, in the face of unrelenting pressure, and he won some and lost some. Don Drysdale went to manager Alston and offered to pitch with two days' rest for the remainder of the season. When the starters faltered, Roebuck, Sherry, and young Perranoski were tossed into the battle.

It was a young club, so it had resilience and strength and the courage of the young. But youth is afflicted in certain ways older men are not. Veteran ballplayers are accustomed to the heat of pennant races, and to the vagaries of fate,

striking down a healthy superstar just when he is most needed. If the young are physically resilient, the more seasoned are mentally resilient.

The Giants, up in San Francisco, had their own problems. Juan Marichal suffered a sliced instep on September 5, and was virtually useless the rest of the way. Jim Davenport was hit by a Drysdale pitched ball, his hand broken, and he was lost for two weeks. Willie Mays fainted in the dugout in Cincinnati, and was hospitalized for four days. The Giants lost all 4 games.

It was a streaky, nervous league. The Giants won 5 in a row early in August, 3 against the Dodgers, and then they lost 6 of their next 7. Were they choking? The Dodgers won 12 of 14, going into early August, and then dropped 5 in a row. Or were they?

Into September the two wounded clubs staggered; the Giants won 7 in a row, and trailed by half a game. Then they lost 6 in a row, and the deficit was 4.

In the seesaw struggle, Koufax—most wounded of all the wounded—felt the pressure close in. In 1955 and 1956, while the Dodgers were winning pennants, little was expected of him. He was just a wild kid, learning his trade. Now, in 1962, he began to sense eyes straying over to him, a silent but urgent plea that somehow he get well quickly and restore order to the chaos of the pennant race.

"It was an awfully helpless feeling," Koufax has since related, "knowing the club needed me and not being able to do anything."

He gave it a whirl the last ten days of the campaign. He had been working out in September, but it was like showing up for spring training all over again. He had to test his finger, not throw too hard (or risk a sore arm or shoulder); he had to sharpen his control; he had to try throwing curves with his raw fingertip. And all the time, there were the Giants, waiting in the wings for the final Dodger collapse.

On September 21, Koufax made his first start in over two months, in St. Louis. The Dodgers were 3 games ahead, with 9 to play. Koufax was opposed by Curt Simmons. The Cardinals had just dropped 8 games in a row, and were in sixth place. The Giants were in Houston for 3 games. In a league where suddenly the front-runners were as much patsies as the second-division clubs, nobody was breathing easy over the assignments.

The Cardinals clobbered Koufax. Rusty, wild, not as fast as he had been, his curve coming in high, Sandy filled the bases in an early inning. Strong, right-handed Charley James jumped on a Koufax curve that hung on the outside corner, chest high, and drove it far over the pavilion roof in right field for a grand-slam home run. The final score: 11–2. In Houston, the Giants won, 11–5. Willie Mays had four hits; he was obviously over his nervous exhaustion.

On September 27, Sandy made another try, this time against Houston. The season had four games to go, and the two leaders had swapped rivals. Now the Giants played St. Louis.

Koufax lasted a bit longer this time. He pitched five innings, but the Colt hitters roughed him up. The Colts

won, 8–6. The Cards beat the Giants, and the Dodgers still led by two games, with three games to go. The next day, Charley James was back again, beating the Dodgers with a run-producing single in the tenth inning of a bitter 3–2 contest. With the Giants idled, the lead was one and a half.

The Dodgers were not to win another game during the regular season. The Giants, staggering but alive, won two of three. Nor could you blame it on the overtaxed Dodger pitchers. Now it was the hitters who failed.

Ernie Broglio shut out the Dodgers, 2–0, on September 29. Curt Simmons shut them out, 1–0, the next day. Catcher Gene Oliver pumped a John Podres fast ball over the left field wall in the eighth inning. In San Francisco, Willie Mays hit a home run off Dick Farrell, and the Giants won a cliffhanger, 2–1.

And the Dodgers and Giants were tied. After 162 games, each had won 101, lost 61. In three days, they would have to do it all over again.

Time cures most ills, most griefs. But there wasn't enough time to cure a sore finger and its aftermath. The exhausted Dodger staff, hanging on by threads, needed a day or two to gather up its strength before meeting the Giant bats. They had no day or two. They got into their private Electra jet-prop job, and flew up to San Francisco on October 1, and then down to Los Angeles on October 2, and, if needed, October 3. The best two-out-of-three would win it, and the right to meet the rested, complacent Yankees in the World Series.

If the Dodgers were tired, so were the Giants. Tired and

worn out by the struggle to catch up. Willie Mays again appeared on the verge of exhaustion. Orlando Cepeda swung a bat that seemed too heavy. Davenport had the flu.

But the name of the game is pitching.

They tossed in Sandy Koufax up in Candlestick Park against the Giants, who were leading from strength with Billy Pierce, undefeated all season at home.

Koufax had beaten the Giants in a vital ball game in July, relying on one pitch.

This time he had none.

The fast ball wasn't very fast. The curve wouldn't curve. His control was wobbly; when he had to come in, he came in "fat"—throwing a medium-speed pitch through the heart of the strike zone.

There were 32,660 hysterical Giant fans in Candlestick Park that afternoon. They saw a massacre.

In the first inning, Koufax got the first two batters, Harvey Kuenn and Chuck Hiller. But Felipe Alou, an old Dodger nemesis, doubled, and Willie Mays timed a Koufax fast ball and hit it out of the park for two runs. In the second frame, Jim Davenport led off with a home run, and when Ed Bailey—who usually has trouble with lefties—ripped a base hit, manager Alston walked to the mound, head down, and Koufax was through for the year.

He had yielded four hits and three runs in one inning plus.

The Dodger relief pitching failed—though it didn't matter—and the Giants banged away. Mays was the big gun,

with three hits in three tries, two of them home runs. He scored three, knocked in three, and stole a base. Pierce held the Dodgers to two singles and a pinch-hit double by Doug Camilli. Big Frank Howard struck out three times.

"I couldn't throw the fast ball," a despondent Koufax said after the game. "The finger was raw. There was no skin on it where you grip the ball. I couldn't grip it across the seams."

The teams moved to Los Angeles. You know the rest. The Dodgers won the longest nine-inning ball game on record, 8–7, with a seven-run burst in the sixth inning. The Giants won it all, 6–4, on October 3, with a four-run rally in the ninth when there was no relief pitching available. The loss of Koufax reached its ultimate consequence in the ninth inning of the third game of a play-off series. Roebuck wore out. Stan Williams could not get the ball over. The Giants scored on bases on balls, infield hits, a sacrifice fly, and an error. Dodger fans were more than disappointed. They were mortified, ashamed. The term used most commonly to describe the Dodgers was choke-up. Eleven years earlier, to the very day, Bob Thomson had driven his home run into the left field seats of the Polo Grounds in a similar play-off. Lightning had struck twice. Memory festered.

"They do not deserve to play in a World Series," Jimmy Cannon wrote.

But more detached observers knew the score. The score was 32. A 32 that had become 0. Sandy Koufax's number. The man with the golden arm that had turned to tin. Had

Koufax not been injured, he would have won at least one ball game that had been lost. One game and there would have been no play-off, no chance to question the Dodgers' courage. Koufax was the difference.

Even with his September record, Koufax still led the league in earned runs, with a 2.54 ERA. He had struck out 216 batters in 184 innings, better than a strikeout an inning, better than 10 a game. Sitting out nearly half a season, Koufax came close to leading the league in strikeouts. Not until the final two weeks did Don Drysdale pass Koufax. Once again Koufax gave up the fewest hits per nine innings —6.55. Big Bob Gibson was a close second, with 6.69.

The Associated Press placed Koufax on its All-National League team, with teammate Drysdale.

With these marks, it is easy to see where the Dodgers stumbled, and why. One need not be a psychologist. Dodger vice-president Fresco Thompson scoffed at reports that manager Alston had not led his club wisely in the stretch.

"When we lost Koufax," Thompson said, "Walt had to go to war with a popgun."

And Al Dark, manager of the winning Giants, said: "If they'd had Sandy all the way, it would have been a different story."

But the psychologists kept probing, and it was finally decided—against all good sense—that the Dodgers had lost because Durocher and Alston had feuded (as they had feuded), because the young players choked (they had undoubtedly not come through in the dying weeks), because

—well, because they were the Dodgers, and the Dodgers did not deserve to win. The question asked around the league as 1962 closed its doors was whether the Dodgers could possibly recover from the collapse of '62. A slogan reminiscent of the past began to shape up.

Wait 'till next year! Then you'll *really* see a collapse.

10

"I Made a Pretty Good Jackass of Myself"

FOR WANT of a nail—poet George Herbert tells us—the shoe is lost; for want of a shoe the horse is lost; for want of a horse, the rider is lost.

For want of a fingertip, the hand was lost. For want of a hand, the man was lost. For want of the man, the team was lost. The team, a pennant, a Series, a fortune—all lost.

All because of a fingertip.

The harpies of baseball are a practical lot. They think in terms of dollars and cents, not victories and losses. When the World Series shifted from a probable location in Los Angeles to a certain site in San Francisco, the amateur accountants got out their scratch pads. The loss to Los Angeles was ultimately reckoned at twelve million dollars.

Innkeepers, restaurateurs, cabbies, car-rental agencies, parking-lot managers, liquor-store owners, and night-club proprietors "lost" the patronage of thousands of potential Angelenos, and visitors, celebrating the Series. The financial loss to the club treasury and the players was estimated at another $850,000. To say nothing of the loss of endorsement monies that accrue almost automatically to pennant

winners. And that free fried chicken on the banquet circuit. All for the loss of a man's fingertip.

You may pay tribute to the little Dutch boy with his finger in the dike. You may recall lucky Jack Horner who shoved a thumb willy-nilly into a pie, and plucked out a juicy plum. You may remember how vividly Dick Nixon waved a finger in the face of Nikita Khrushchev, and the world marveled.

Fingers have played a vital part in history and legend. The knitting fingers of the women at the site of beheadings, in the French revolution. The sensitive flying fingers of Annie Sullivan and Helen Keller, communicating through a world of black silence.

The fingers that squeezed triggers and snuffed out the lives of archdukes, kings, and presidents. The finger of Emile Zola, shaken in the face of French injustice in the Dreyfuss case. The downturned thumbs of spectators at gladiatorial circuses, that meant death. The upturned thumb that granted life. Winston Churchill's V for victory.

In the face of such fingers, Sandy Koufax's sore index digit takes on more limited significance. It was, after all, just a ballplayer's malfunctioning finger. It cost Los Angeles twelve million dollars, but the world did not change its course.

Still, we are a nation of sports fans, and as 1963 began to inch its way through history, people who would meet or hear about or read about or think about Sandy Koufax would invariably ask or wonder:

"How is the finger?"

It had become *the* finger. If you had played free association with the average American in early 1963 and said, "Finger," he would have said: "Sandy Koufax."

Sandy Koufax took his finger on the road with him. He joined a troupe of other Dodgers, Duke Snider, Don Drysdale, Maury Wills, Frank Howard, and Willie Davis, in a night-club act (and some of the $12-million started coming back), headed by Milton Berle, at the Desert Inn in Las Vegas. For a month, Sandy cavorted onstage with his teammates, receiving a neat $8,000 for the work, and supplying the act's biggest laugh nightly.

Milton Berle would ask Sandy: "How's the finger?"

"It's great," Koufax would say (and the audience would warmly and generously applaud), and then he would add: "All I've got now is a little problem with my thumb." He would hold up a huge thumb, bandaged with plastic and rubber.

Koufax and Berle and the rest took the act to the Fontainebleau Hotel in Miami for eleven more nights, two shows nightly, and several more thousand dollars, and always the biggest laugh provoker was Sandy Koufax and his huge swollen thumb.

Offstage, it wasn't so funny. Nobody knew for sure how the finger really was. It felt fine, but would it stand up under the heavy activity of spinning off curves, swinging bats, throwing fast balls?

"It feels all right," Koufax said in the early days of spring

training at Vero Beach, Florida. "I don't think it's going to give me any trouble. I've been to the doctor, and he says it shouldn't bother me."

But nobody knew for sure. And finally Sandy Koufax evolved a quiplike answer for the monotonous question that always greeted him: "How's the finger?"

"Fine," Sandy would say. "Wanna go out and play some catch?" And the picture of a well-meaning soft-handed spectator suddenly forced to catch a Koufax fast ball—sore finger or no—soon put an end to *that* interview.

The finger did seem fine. It felt fine, which was important, because when the finger was bad, it felt neither fine nor ill. It felt nothing. It was numb, the blood shut off. Now there was full feeling in the hand. The circulation that had been measured at a drippy 15 percent was now up to a robustly cascading 85 percent—normal.

Sandy expounded a bit to writer Robert Creamer.

"The clot is gone," he said. "I honestly don't expect to have any trouble, though I won't know definitely until I've thrown hard for a while. I'm sure the clot won't come back, and the circulation should be O.K." Then he touched on a phase of the problem that remained unknown. "The only thing is, we don't know what damage might have been done to the finger when the circulation was bad. There might be damaged cells or something like that, and that might show up when I start to throw hard."

Sandy smiled a resigned smile and said: "I'll have to wait and see."

Then Koufax was off to enjoy himself briefly before the season settled in, before facing the grim question. He played golf in the annual ballplayers' tournament at Miami Springs Country Club. He is an ambidextrous golfer—that is, he putts righty, but plays every other club left-handed. There is an explanation for such seeming confusion. The muscles of Koufax's left arm and shoulder are so thickly developed that his backswing would be severely restricted, were he to swing right-handed. The explanation did not satisfy everyone. "Boy, you're all mixed up," Maury Wills scoffed. Wills might have been right. Koufax golfs up in the 90s.

Then the golf was over, and baseball began. This was the testing grounds. In 1962, Koufax had received a salary close to but not reaching $30,000. After his great, but aborted, season, Buzzie Bavasi raised the left-hander to around $35,000. Yet everyone in baseball knew that were Koufax "right," he could not only become the highest-paid Dodger, but might soon threaten the $75,000 salaries paid Warren Spahn and Bob Feller.

Koufax worked carefully at Vero Beach. The pressure was enormous, and occasionally Koufax indicated his discomfort. "I just don't want anyone to say everything depends on me. I just want to pitch the best I can for the team and then be able to leave the park and be left alone."

All eyes were riveted on the handsome hurler. Gradually he was becoming a national idol. The clusters of autograph seekers kept growing until they were mobs. Demands on Koufax's time—interviews, endorsements, phone calls, pub-

lic appearances—increased. It is, at first, exhilarating, heady, this acclaim. Then it tends to become monotonous. Finally it grows into an irritant. Few men are geared to take it with equanimity. Stan Musial was one of the few. Others react violently. Koufax is a middle man in this range, neither as astonishingly equable as Musial, nor as vitriolic as —well, as others.

But no matter what, the problem was playing baseball. All else faded. He worked, at Vero Beach. But the work and the national interest dovetailed. Koufax suffered a minor blood blister on his pitching hand. Everybody had to see; the writers queued up for interviews. He tore a fingernail, and it went out on the press association wires.

Koufax had been given an unexpected bonus. On January 26, 1963, the baseball rules-makers had decided to expand the strike zone. The top limit of the zone was raised from the level of the armpits to the top of a batter's shoulders. Not a pitcher in the league would grant that the strike zone had been a help in 1963, but for all the Mayses and Aarons and Killebrews, the year was a pitcher's year. The fast ball fired chest high and hopping had to be a called strike. Silent or not, disavowing or not, the big fireball throwers had to be delighted. It was a rule written for them.

Koufax needs no help from the rules-makers. His ability to throw a baseball into a strike zone no bigger than an umpire's heart had been proved over the past two seasons. But the fact remains, rules men had given him three or four inches of breathing space.

In the spring of 1963, Sandy Koufax—always a two-pitch pitcher, with a rare change-up for an occasional third pitch—began experimenting on a slider. A slider, for the few uninitiated, has become the pitch of modern times. It is a curve ball delivered by permitting the baseball to roll or slide off the side of the fingers, instead of unloosing the ball with a violent twist of wrist and arm. A slider curves on a flat lateral plane; a pure curve not only curves laterally, it invariably breaks down. Old-timers called the slider a "nickel curve." But modern-day pitchers value it highly. There are some hitters, Stan Musial, for one, who insist the slider is now baseball's most effective pitch. When Warren Spahn realized his fast ball had lost some of its zing, he turned to two new pitches—a screwball and a slider. His effectiveness increased.

Koufax does not need a slider. Yet. But he began looking ahead, in the spring of '63, to the day he might need a fuller bag of tricks. Perhaps the injury of '62 had given Koufax time to pause and face his future. A disabled man often takes stock. Koufax may have learned that things happen to a man, even the youngest and strongest among us. So you prepare. You cover all exits. He worked on a slider.

The Dodgers of 1963 were co-favorites with the Giants to win the pennant. The team was young, strong, swift, and determined. But a scar remained. No one knew how deep it ran, inside. Not the scar of Koufax's index finger. The scar of defeat, of collapse, perhaps of self-doubt.

Spring training was an odd experience. The Dodgers

were edgy. Players complained over minor incidents. You could say—had you known how it all turned out—that the edginess was a sign of a well-tuned athlete, ready to go. Or, had it worked out disastrously, you could have said: See, dissension has cut out the heart of this club.

But you didn't know. Nobody knew.

The facts were ominous. Players began to complain to Buzzie Bavasi about manager Alston. Not many players, not many complaints, and none of them of much substance. But Bavasi sensed that the complaints were symptomatic of a greater ailment.

Bavasi took charge. In Chicago, where the season opened for the Dodgers in the second week of April, 1963, Bavasi called a closed clubhouse meeting, and the Los Angeles general manager decided to accept the role of scapegoat for the 1962 debacle.

According to Bob Hunter, in an exclusive story for the Los Angeles *Herald-Examiner*, Bavasi said, in a choking voice:

"None of you are responsible for what happened at the end of last season. The guy to blame is—Bavasi." He tapped his chest.

The thinking behind Bavasi's self-accusation is this: The Dodgers carried nine pitchers in 1962. When Koufax was lost, eight pitchers were not enough to heft the load. Bavasi did not call up enough pitching help from the minors; he did not deal for help elsewhere, to replace Koufax and to spell out the starting trio of Drysdale, Podres, and Williams.

But last year was last year. "If you lose this year," Bavasi reputedly told his players, "you won't be blamed, and Alston won't be blamed. I will be blamed. No one else."

And then in a dramatic confrontation, Bavasi demanded his players stand, one at a time, and declare whether each thought the team could win the '63 pennant. The effect was a little like a Knute Rockne half-time pep talk. The Dodgers burst onto Wrigley Field that afternoon, ready to chew nails. Drysdale mowed down the Cubs, though he had to rub down his pitching arm frequently to keep it warm, so frigid was the weather.

The Bavasi clubhouse lecture had some effect. But the general manager is no magician, and the discontent that he shrewdly sensed lay beneath the surface, soon came bubbling up. The team started off raggedly, playing at a .500 clip, while the Giants and Cards were winning. Nor was it a case of worrying over Sandy Koufax. Koufax was pitching well.

Well? On the second day of the season, Sandy threw a five-hitter against the Cubs, beating them, 2–1. Then on April 19 at Los Angeles, Koufax shut out the Houston Colts, 2–0. He gave up just two hits. His finger felt fine. The fast ball was exploding. The curve could cut butter. The change was a tantalizing butterfly.

Everything was fine.

Then Sandy Koufax dropped a bomb.

"I have a pain in my left shoulder that keeps getting worse," he said. Back into the repair pits he went.

The pain was burrowed into the posterior capsule of his left shoulder, a hollow where the upper arm bone fits into the shoulder blade. Doctors thought Sandy had either stretched or torn a membrane covering the muscles located in the area of the capsule. Koufax was laid up nearly two weeks. He missed three turns.

The club was not playing well. In the first days of May the Dodgers slipped into fifth place, 5 games behind the leaders.

On Sunday, May 6, the Dodgers dropped a ball game to Pittsburgh and when the team got on a bus to drive to the Pittsburgh airport, they were seventh. The bus the team rode that afternoon had seen better days, but it apparently was the best traveling secretary Lee Scott had been able to line up for the ride.

Disgruntled at the day's loss, pessimistic because of the standings, the players began to grumble aloud. Then—it happened. The Pirate squad, also leaving Pittsburgh, breezed past the Dodger bus, and the Los Angeles players stared enviously at the modern air-conditioned vehicle carrying the enemy to the airport. The players began to snarl abuse at Lee Scott. Scott answered back.

Suddenly, from a seat near the front of the bus, Walter Alston stood up. Alston is a powerful man, and a patient man. He is a man who says little, but who says much. He is a rural man with an urbane wit. He is a man who once said of managing: "In this business, it is not a matter of will you get fired, but when."

If this is his philosophy, Walt Alston has it made, because he has little to lose except time. If you are fatalistic about your future, you can take chances a more hopeful man would never dare. There is a word to be said for pessimism.

And there were words to be said in the bus that Sunday. Alston said them. He ordered the bus driver to pull to the side of the road. He spoke his piece, briefly, angrily, forcefully. This was *his* club. If you had a complaint to make, make it to him. And *he* tapped his chest. His chest is thicker than Bavasi's. There would be no more griping. (And Alston didn't mean just bus-griping; he is no fool; he knew what had been going on all that spring.) Did the players understand? If they didn't understand, he'd be glad to step outside with any—or all—of them, and explain it more fully.

Nobody stirred. Silence settled over the busload of weary dispirited ballplayers. This was no pep talk.

But it may have done the job more than any amount of stand-up-and-be-counted locker-room histrionics.

The Dodgers needed no emotional lift. What they needed was the exact opposite. A touch of composure. A moment where they could settle down and indulge in that rarity for athletes—a bit of introspection. Reason could have told them they were the finest team in baseball. No team ever ran as well. The pitching was overpowering. The hitting was sharp, if not equally overpowering. The defense was as tight as a submarine berth.

Facts were on their side. The Giants had been lucky to

win in '62. The Dodgers had lost their finest pitcher, and still came within an inning of winning. The Giants were now plagued with problems, factual problems. Billy Pierce was a year older. Instead of winning just about every game, he was losing just about every game. Sanford, a year older, was obviously not going to win 24. The relief pitching was not to be trusted. And if the Dodgers suffered from self-doubt, the Giants suffered a worse disease: overconfidence. At their training camp in Arizona, the Giants looked like fat cats, sleek and smiling. The San Francisco press corps was contemptuous of the Dodger chances in '63. The Dodgers would be lucky to finish fourth, they said.

The moment of composure helped settle the Dodgers. Tension eased out. They started to win. Sandy Koufax discovered one day his shoulder had stopped hurting. It was—he thought—an adhesion that had now ripped loose. He felt fine, strong, ready. "I guess I'm just getting old," he joshed. "Falling apart, piece by piece." Laughter was the catalyst, not melodrama and fear. Koufax proved his fitness. He beat the Cardinals, 11–1, with a five-hitter.

On May 11, 1963, Koufax proved it again, and nailed it down for all time. It was Ladies' Night at Dodger Stadium. A squealing throng of 55,530 fans turned out, the park's absolute capacity. Among them were Koufax's mother and father, watching their son pitch. It was a rare experience for them. It became even rarer.

Through seven innings, Koufax retired 21 Giants in order. There was an occasional sharply hit ball, but never a

near-hit. Harvey Kuenn looped a line drive to right field, where Frank Howard stood in his tracks and swallowed it. Felipe Alou lofted a long fly to left field, but Tommy Davis had room to spare in front of the fence, to make the catch. Willie Mays hit a line drive down the third-base line, but he hit it off his handle, jammed by a fast ball, and he hit it straight at Jim Gilliam.

Bill Libby, a perceptive sportswriter, was at Dodger Stadium that night, for *Sport* magazine. He tells how the tension grew in the late innings, as it always grows in no-hitters. Rookie Dick Calmus stood up in the Dodger dugout to applaud Koufax as the Giants went down in the seventh. Leo Durocher curtly ordered the boy to sit down. Did he want to jinx things?

From a seat behind the dugout, a youngster piped to Koufax as he walked to the bench that inning: "Hey, Sandy, you gonna pitch me a no-hitter?"

Jinx-oriented Leo Durocher made a face.

Sandy Koufax smiled grimly and said to himself, *I hope to God so.*

Ed Bailey broke the perfecto, drawing Koufax's first base on balls in the eighth inning, but the next man hit into a double play, and still the Giants had no hits. Into the ninth the lean left-hander worked, against the league's most power-packed lineup, chockful of right-handed sluggers. The Dodgers were going to win the game, no matter what. They had scored a run in the second, blown the game apart in the sixth with three more, and iced the cake with four in the eighth. As the Giants took their last licks, it was 8–0,

although Koufax had momentarily forgotten those last four runs. He went into his windup, thinking he had a four-run lead. If men got on, and the bases were loaded, he'd be in trouble. Later that inning, he glanced behind him at the scoreboard and saw it was really 8–0. The relief was a splendid stimulant.

First, the weak sisters, who somehow always seem to be the men who break up no-hitters. Joe Amalfitano and Jose Pagan. But they both went down meekly, and Koufax was a single out away from his second no-hitter.

The hitter was Willie McCovey, batting for the pitcher. McCovey chews up Dodger pitching. In his rookie year in '59, he had hit a home run off Koufax that this observer still recalls, a gigantic unswerving line drive, close to the foul line at the Los Angeles Coliseum, and crashing into the seats, a mammoth shot that rocketed off his bat and never lost a speck of its velocity.

Koufax walked McCovey.

Now the hitter was Harvey Kuenn. Kuenn is one of the tougher men in the league to strike out. He gets a piece of wood on the pitch. A piece of wood can mean a blooper over the infield, a ball squiggled past an infielder. Koufax's face was grimy with sweat. His beard was dark. In the white lights of Dodger Stadium, he was all black and white, black brows and black hollows for eyes, a white blade of bone for a nose and white cheekbones glistening with oily sweat, a black smudge beneath his nose and another smudge coating his chops. His throat was a black shadow.

He stretched and threw, and Kuenn topped the ball to

the second-base side of the mound. Koufax rushed over, gobbled up the bounder, started to run toward first and then awkwardly half lobbed and half pushed the ball underhanded to Ron Fairly, well ahead of Kuenn.

Koufax continued his run to first, leaped on Fairly, and the 55,000 fans, many of them incoherent females, babbled their delight.

Koufax had his second no-hitter. He struck out just four men. Yet seldom, if ever, has he pitched with greater skill. He credited John Roseboro with calling "a brilliant game." He called the effort "my greatest thrill." He glowingly recalled the standing ovation tendered him when he batted in the eighth. He said he was "very happy, very happy."

If 1962 provided a great first half-year, this 1963 was even better. Eight days after the Giant no-hitter, Koufax blanked the Mets, 1–0, on two hits. Nine days later at Milwaukee, he blanked the Braves—a team that often gives him misery—7–0, on six hits. The team rumbled into June, and Koufax kept dipping into the can of fresh whitewash. On June 13, it was a three-hit job against Houston, the Dodgers winning 3–0. Four days later, Sandy was up in San Francisco, edging the Giants, 2–0, on four hits.

On July 2, Don Drysdale shut out the Cards, 1–0, and Los Angeles replaced St. Louis as the league leader. The Dodgers were never headed, but, my, it got sticky. It always does get sticky, around the Dodgers.

The next day, Koufax shut out St. Louis, 5–0, on three singles. The lead increased. Four days later, nearing the

All-Star break, Sandy blanked Cincinnati, 4–0, and again he gave up but three hits.

But nothing is ever easy in baseball. The Dodgers released a pair of veterans, Don Zimmer, the fiery infielder, and Ed Roebuck, the phlegmatic reliever whose stony face had masked his emotions for so long his teammates and even his manager had come to assume he had no emotions.

Not surprisingly, Zimmer unloosed a blast at the Dodger front office and manager Alston. Quite surprisingly, Roebuck fired a second salvo. The word "dissension" was spoken out loud again, and dire warnings were issued of impending Dodger collapse, of another "choke" session.

Koufax ran his record to 16-and-3, better than his mark at the same period a year before. His earned-run average was 1.75, which comes close to the vanishing point. He had 14 complete games, 9 of them shutouts. He'd even won a ball game against Milwaukee by hitting a three-run home run. He was Baseball Joe, Frank Merriwell, Jack Armstrong. And America's fandom came out of their living rooms to pack ball parks where Sandy Koufax pitched. Not since Dizzy Dean had a National League pitcher so gripped the imagination of the fans. In Philadelphia, reported Jack Olsen, in *Sports Illustrated,* a Dodger-Philly game was Standing Room Only by four in the afternoon. Why? Koufax would pitch. The official attendance was 35,353. Connie Mack Stadium seats just 33,166. Over 15,000 were turned away. Veteran Philadelphia observers said it was the greatest turnaway crowd they'd ever seen.

Koufax had become a huge drawing card. In 1963 the Dodgers drew 2,538,602 fans, the only club to go over two million. The defending Giants were almost a million fans back. Koufax cannot be credited with all of this, of course, but it has been estimated that his presence on the mound entices an additional 7,000 fans into the home park and as many as 15,000 extra fans when the Dodgers are on the road.

Nor was it because he was the only super-pitcher in the league. Juan Marichal of the Giants was pitching nearly as well, with his own no-hitter thrown in. Dick Ellsworth, a young left-hander with the lowly Cubs, was having a magnificent year. So were Jim Maloney and Bob Friend.

But only Koufax captured the imagination this way. If there is a reason (other than the fact he was a better pitcher in '63 than any of these other fine pitchers) it probably lies in the way we admire the wounded who come back. It is no trick to win when you are bigger and stronger and faster and wiser than anybody else. The trick, then, is to lose. But when your physical assets are not a whit different, and when you suffer an injury that threatens not only your immediate effectiveness, but your whole career, then you become something else again. Joe DiMaggio, crippled, crawling off the Yankee bench to beat back Boston's pennant bid with a cluster of home runs. Carl Hubbell, coming back from an elbow-chip operation, and overage, pitching his one-hit shutout of the Dodgers in 1940, facing the minimum 27 batters. Duke Snider, playing with a knee that fires off burst-

ing pain when he swings a bat and runs the bases. Mickey Mantle.

Not that Sandy Koufax, in 1963, was a wounded man, overcoming his handicaps. He'd obviously already overcome. Less and less did you hear the question: "How's the finger?" The finger was fine. There was a bit of scar tissue on the tip. Sometimes it got tender. Inside, Koufax could feel a tiny hard spot. That was all.

By August 1, the Dodgers opened a 4½-game lead over the Giants, 5 over the Cards. On August 3, down in Houston, Koufax recorded his tenth shutout, far and away ahead of anybody else in the game. It was another masterpiece, a three-hitter. The Dodgers won, 2–0. It was the fifth shutout in which the Dodgers had provided Sandy with three runs or fewer. Nothing was easy.

The pennant race continued warm, if not hot. The Giants were not the club they were a year before. But the Cards, sparked by Dick Groat and a rejuvenated Stan Musial, and paced by topflight pitchers Bob Gibson, Curt Simmons, and Ernie Broglio, refused to lie still. Down in the second division, the Phils began to stir.

On August 15, Koufax made his final appearance of the year in Milwaukee. Gene Oliver, the old Dodger killer, smashed a three-run home run in the first inning, and Koufax was driven out. Ron Perranoski won in relief, but the rumormongers were at it again. Was it the finger? Or a new ailment in the arm or shoulder?

Koufax was nettled. "Sure the Braves blasted me," he

said. "Why make a federal case of it if I don't pitch a shutout, or even pitch very good in every start?"

It was a good question. Koufax was great, but he had not as yet achieved the impossible. In every game somebody would hit a pitch, fair or foul. You can't retire three men on nine pitches, every inning of every game.

Five times Koufax failed to finish ball games against Milwaukee. "They're a tough club for a left-hander," Koufax explained. "They keep sending right-handed batters up against you, and you can't make many mistakes."

He had made some mistakes in this August 15 game, but it wasn't a question of Koufax faltering. In the stretch, he was better than ever. His month-by-month record proves it. He won 2 games in April and lost 1; in May it was 5-and-1; in June, 5-and-1; in July 5-and-1; in August 3-and-1; and he closed out the season with five wins and no losses in September. In no month did he lose more than a single ball game.

But there were moments. Sandy Koufax told Milton Gross about them. He said he still made lots of mistakes.

"I get so frustrated I don't know what to do," he admitted. "I may take it out on the water cooler or tip over the rubbing table or throw a wastebasket against the wall." Two things upset Koufax. If he pitched poorly, he would be sore at himself. If he pitched well, but the team didn't hit and he had to be removed for a pinch hitter, the good job down the drain, he got sore at a scapegoat known as Fate. He told Gross he'd made a shambles of the clubhouse a few times in '63. He remembered a game in Chicago he'd acted "like a

kid" and continued childishly in the dugout and in the clubhouse, because he'd been removed from a tight ball game. In San Francisco, he told how he'd nearly torn the dressing-room door off its hinges before he got inside. "I made a pretty good jackass of myself."

A moment of edginess occurred late in August. The Dodgers and Koufax were going along swimmingly. Behind them, the Cards had not yet worked up any real momentum. But there was uneasiness. In 1951, the Dodgers had led by 13½ on August 10, and still had lost. They had led by 4 with a week to play in 1962, and had lost. Now the lead opened up to 5 or 6 games, and then slimmed back down to 3. It was a steady lead, but the Dodgers were not able to break the league wide open. In San Francisco, manager Dark tried to unsettle his down-state rivals. He reminded everybody of the past year's chronology. He pointed to the number of games remaining between the Giants and the Dodgers.

Whatever the reason, some Dodgers began to play ball with their heads turned back, looking over their shoulders. The pitchers began to buckle under the strain. It never reached the stage of revolt or even real bickering, but some of the Dodger pitchers began to complain of overwork. On the squad was a young talented bonus boy named Dick Calmus, just nineteen years old. Dodger pitchers, abetted by the press, began to urge that manager Alston use young Calmus, and give everybody else a day of rest. Sandy Koufax said:

"I wish at nineteen that *I'd* known what Dick Calmus

knows about pitching. He has a definite idea when he takes the mound."

On August 23, 1963, Walt Alston sent Dick Calmus to the mound against the Braves.

Strong men blanched. Others ducked, to avoid the shrapnel. The carnage was awful. In two-thirds of an inning, Calmus gave up four hits, all of them line shots, and two runs. The last was a bullet fired straight back to the box, striking Calmus on the leg and all but tearing it loose. The youngster limped off the mound, and the Braves went on to win, 6–1.

Now the press second-guessed Alston. Why had he chosen to send the boy against the man-eating Braves?

Dryly, Alston said: "There aren't many virgins in the league I can send him against."

The Dodgers lost again the next day, and then Sandy Koufax, the team stopper, pitched into the ninth inning of a ball game, leading 2–1, when he either did or didn't get tired. Alston came to the mound to replace him.

In frustrated anger, Koufax ran from the mound, stopping for a moment behind second base as though he wanted to hide from Alston. Then he stormed into the dugout.

Explained Alston: "He was tired."

Replied Koufax to the press: "I was not."

To sports columnist Sid Ziff, Sandy seemed "deeply disturbed and disappointed. He wanted people to know it. He was angry and upset."

Buzzie Bavasi, that old quorum-caller, got the players

and coaches together, and warned them that second-guessing Alston and criticizing him in public would not be tolerated.

That was all. Koufax returned to his relatively equable nature. Harmony was restored. On August 29, the Giants came to town, and Al Dark tried to repeat his formula of last year when he predicted his club would beat the Dodgers five of the remaining seven times they met. The Giants actually won six of seven. Now Dark said the magic words and waved his wand.

"Five of seven," he grimly vowed.

He must have conceded the first right off. He sent young, even more erratic, and far more scatter-gunned Bob Bolin against Koufax in the opener. The Dodgers climbed all over Bolin while Koufax was toying with the Giants. The final score was 11–1.

It was a landmark triumph in more ways than one. Dodger publicist, Arther E. (Red) Patterson, an old-time dog-show fancier, had started to look like an untrimmed poodle. Patterson had decided not to have his hair cut until the light-hitting Dodgers scored at least four runs in a single inning. On August 29, the Dodgers did it, and Red Patterson was shorn.

But less trivially, Sandy Koufax won his twentieth game. No pitcher had won as many. After the easy win, Dodger broadcaster Jerry Doggett said to Koufax: "This makes up for all the games when you didn't get any runs, doesn't it?"

"No," said Koufax, "it doesn't."

But Koufax was winging, and so were the Dodgers as they swept into September and buried the Giants. They beat San Francisco three out of four, and every Los Angeles fan chortled: "Now Dark will have to win four out of three."

The Giants was, or were, dead. But the Cards were, or was, not. If the Dodgers were warming to the task, the Cardinals were boiling. Johnny Keane's club suddenly could not lose. They set off on a 9-game winning streak. When it ended, they would then win 10 in a row more.

On Labor Day, Koufax won his 21st, 7–3, over Houston, in which he struck out 13 and walked nobody. But the Cards kept winning, and unexpected tragedies struck the Dodgers. Don Drysdale had to attend a friend's funeral. Maury Wills flew home to Spokane because his wife had delivered a stillborn child. But Willie Davis lifted the gloom. He got married, and announced he'd take no honeymoon now. "We'll spend our honeymoon in New York, while we're in the World Series."

On September 6, Koufax beat the Giants up in Candlestick Park, for his 22nd win. It was a must triumph. For all their burial, the Giants didn't die that easy. Up in San Francisco, they beat the Dodgers two out of three, and feelings were so tense, Giant and Dodger writers staged a fist fight in the press box.

Personal tragedy continued to dog the Dodgers. This time, Sandy's dad, Irving Koufax, suffered a mild heart seizure. Sandy flew home, to spend a few days with his folks, until he was assured his father was recovering nicely.

Then Koufax rejoined the Dodgers, in time for the big final eastern swing through the league.

The pennant race had suddenly become a humdinger. The Cards were charging. The Dodgers opened in Pittsburgh, and on September 10, Koufax went against the Pirates. The Pirate fans came out, not to root for the home team, but to root against the Dodgers. The entire nation had seemingly become Cardinal fans. Perhaps it was the sentimental thought of Stan Musial, playing in one last World Series. Perhaps it was our affinity for the underdog. Perhaps it was a hangover of the disdain fans felt for the Dodgers during the 1962 collapse.

In an early inning at Forbes Field, a fan leaned into the Dodger dugout and pointed to the scoreboard: "Hey, look, you guys, the Cards got two in the first, with Gibson pitching."

Don Drysdale stuck his head out. "Yeah," he snapped, "and we got one in the first with Koufax pitching."

Behind Koufax, the Dodgers won, 4–2. Sandy had his 23rd.

But the fan was right as rain. Koufax winning did not shake the Cards loose. They hung on. The Dodgers moved into Philadelphia, and the Los Angeles club started to show its jitters. They played a twi-night twin bill on September 13—Friday the 13th—and in the opener, pitching with two days' rest, Sandy Koufax faced young Chris Short. It was strikeout season that evening. Koufax fanned eight in seven innings, gave up four hits, and just one run.

Short was better. He overpowered the Dodgers. He fanned 14.

In the eighth, trailing 1–0, Koufax retired for a pinch hitter. The Dodgers scored two runs, and it appeared that Sandy was going to win one in the shower. Then in the ninth inning, Don Hoak ran straight up into Maury Wills on a double-play situation, and Wills threw the ball away. Two runs scored, and the Dodgers suffered a crushing defeat, 3–2.

While the Cards kept winning.

The Dodgers had not played badly. Going into the beginning of the critical series in St. Louis, on September 16, the Dodgers had won 13 of their last 19. Better than .667 ball. But the Cards had won 19 of 20.

The lead was one game when Captain Bump Holman set down the Dodger-owned jet-prop Electra II in St. Louis on Monday, September 16. The club was tense. A few days before, Koufax had been asked if he felt "the hot breath of the Cards" on his back.

"Sorry, buddy," said Koufax, rubbing his neck—he loathes such clichés—"I don't feel a thing back there."

Clichés aside, the Dodgers knew they were there. Out at Busch Stadium, before the first game, Dodger pitchers griped about the height of the Cardinal mound. All except Koufax, who liked it high that way. "It helps my overhanded curve ball," he said. It didn't really matter to the others. Every park's mound is slightly different. You get used to it. It takes a pitcher a half-dozen pitches to make

whatever adjustments are necessary. The Dodgers had used the Cardinal mound many times before. They weren't complaining about the mound, as such. They were reacting once again to the fierce unending pressure. They were being human.

But behind the almost gay faces of the Cards, similar tensions were building. No matter what, the Dodgers led. It was up to the Cards to do the catching up. In the four-game set, the Cards *had* to win three. Two would not do the job, and two would put a sizable slowdown in the furious momentum of the past three weeks. Anything less than two wins would be a catastrophe.

Selected to pitch the opener of the series, John Podres announced cockily: "I'll shut 'em out." But even as Walt Alston was saying patiently: "There is no pressure. It's just another game," Podres was telling a writer: "If you don't think there's pressure on me, you're crazy."

In the Card dugout, Lou Burdette clutched his throat, in the ancient sign of the choke-up.

Podres didn't shut them out. Or, rather, he shut out everybody but Stan Musial. Musial hit a home run to tie the game at 1–1. Then the Dodgers scored twice, and won the first game of the series, 3–1. The lead was two games.

Koufax went the next night. In a sense, this was truly the biggest game of the series, and of the season. Writers had posted it even more floridly: "The Game of the Century."

Curt Simmons was going for the Cards. Nobody could remember the last time he had lost. Heck, nobody could re-

member the last time he'd been scored on. Actually, it was twenty-eight innings ago.

Had the Cards won the game, and the next—with their ace Gibson scheduled to go—the pennant race would have been tied. But if Koufax won, the Dodgers had to leave with at least a comfortable two-game lead. Possibly a four-game lead.

Johnny Keane said of Koufax before the game: "He's a great pitcher, but he's only one of quite a few great pitchers in the league, and we've had to beat them all to stay up there."

In the first inning, Maury Wills singled, stole second, went to third on a Simmons' wild pitch, and scored on Jim Gilliam's double.

The game was as good as over.

Koufax hurled his eleventh shutout, and in so doing broke a National League record for shutouts by left-handed pitchers. The man whose record he broke was Carl Hubbell. Koufax had again scratched his way past another great name of baseball legend.

Sandy gave up four hits, all singles. He struck out four. He walked nobody.

Yet there were moments of doubt, even in this 4–0 win. In the third inning with one out, Sandy hit catcher Tim McCarver. Simmons bunted back to the mound, and Koufax threw the ball into center field. There were runners on first and third, and the top of the order coming up.

Julian Javier bounced to Wills. Wills threw to the plate, and Roseboro, the finest catcher since Wes Westrum at

blocking off runners, tagged out the sliding McCarver. Dick Groat tapped back to the mound, and the threat was over.

Koufax had a no-hitter for six innings. In the seventh, Stan Musial singled. There were three meaningless singles the final two frames. Koufax threw exactly 87 pitches that September evening. You barely work up a sweat on 87 pitches. His record stood at 24-and-5.

The next day the Dodgers won, in extra innings, after the Cards had built up a big lead. The word "choke" went out of fashion in Los Angeles.

The Cards kept losing until they were beaten on September 24, and the Dodgers found they had won the pennant before playing the Mets that evening.

Koufax made his last appearance on September 25, against the Mets. It was a glittering tune-up for the World Series. There were Yankee scouts in the stands, and Koufax was a virtuoso. He worked just five innings. The Mets touched him for four hits, no runs. Koufax fanned eight men. Bob Miller and Ron Perranoski tacked on four more shutout innings. The Dodgers won, 1–0.

The eight strikeouts gave Sandy 306 for the season, the first National Leaguer ever to break 300. Only three other men in the modern history of baseball have ever struck out 300 or more men: Rube Waddell, Walter Johnson, and Bob Feller.

All of Sandy's statistics for the pennant year of 1963 are eye-catching. He was one of three pitchers in the league to work 300 or more innings. In forty starts, Sandy pitched 20 complete games. His control was astonishing. In those 311

innings, he walked just 58 men. The year before, he'd walked 57 men in 127 fewer innings.

His earned-run average was 1.88, lowest in the league since Howie Pollet's 1.74 twenty years earlier. He became the first National Leaguer to win the ERA title two years in a row since Cincinnati's Bucky Walters won in 1939 and 1940.

Of his eleven shutouts, one had been the no-hitter. Two were two-hitters, five were three-hitters, two four-hitters, and in the other, he gave up six hits.

He had concluded nine major-league seasons, and his overall record stood at 93 wins and 65 losses. In 1,443 innings he had struck out 1,474, the only starting pitcher in the history of the game to strike out better than a man an inning. His overall earned-run average was 3.26, and shrinking.

But you cannot carry a bagful of statistics onto the mound at Yankee Stadium and expect the New York Yankees to read them and curl up and die.

Nobody beats the Yankees with a reputation. Nobody had ever accused the Yankees of choking. Automatically, without giving it a thought, the oddsmakers installed the Yankees a solid favorite to win the 1963 World Series.

Ralph Houk, Yankee manager, exuded confidence on the eve of the Series:

"We've got a better all-round ball club than the Dodgers. And we're going to win it."

But the Yankees knew of one hurdle. Their chief scout,

Mayo Smith, had watched a young man throw bullets past National League hitters the last few weeks of the season, and next to the name of Sandy Koufax on his scouting report, Smith wrote:

"Simply the best."

11

From Tip to Toe

MAN FOR MAN, it would appear that Ralph Houk was correct in declaring his club the better all-round team. The Yankee infield has been described as the finest defensive unit in many years, perhaps the best ever to play ball.

Joe Pepitone appeared the better first baseman, in the field and at bat, than either aging Bill Skowron—whom the Yankees had unloaded—or young Ron Fairly. At second, the Dodgers were going to have to go with young, untried Dick Tracewski. Tracewski was playing only because Ken McMullen, the Dodger third baseman, had hurt himself the last days of the season, and Jim Gilliam would play third. That left second open. Tracewski would attempt to fill the slot.

Bobby Richardson shaped up as the better man, in the field, at bat, in experience and knowledge, and in any other way two second basemen can be compared.

Tony Kubek has been credited for years now with great range, a strong arm and sure hands, the credentials of a first-class shortstop. He was a sharp, if not devastating hit-

ter. Maury Wills, for all his flash and speed, often comes close to leading the league in errors. He was a pesty hitter, but with little power. At third, Gilliam was not in the class of young Clete Boyer, often touted as the finest fielding third baseman of all time. If Gilliam had an edge it was an intangible thing—his uncanny ability to get on base, to be where he had to be in the field, to move runners up, to make pitchers work, to do all the things that men with limited skills must do if they intend to last in major-league competition. Gilliam had lasted so well he was very much in the running for the league's most valuable player. Nobody would say the same of Clete Boyer, for all his enormous skill.

Yankees outfielders Roger Maris, Mickey Mantle, and Tom Tresh rated solidly over Frank Howard, Willie and Tommy Davis. Behind the plate, Elston Howard was headed for his Most Valuable Player award. Roseboro had never impressed as a great receiver; his hitting had always been faulty.

So there you are.

No place.

You compare teams and players only when they meet head to head, over a long pull. If it is true that the American League is now inferior to the National—as many experts insist—then the Yankee superiority is evident only when compared with inferior clubs. The year before, the Yankees had beaten a totally exhausted Giant team by the length of a base bat—the distance needed for Willie Mc-

Covey's bullet to blur past Bobby Richardson, instead of dying in his frozen glove. And the Giants frankly didn't seem to care. They had won a pennant and play-off nobody expected them to win; the Series was anticlimactic.

Besides, all the comparisons of man to man seldom take into account the value of pitching. A second baseman may be slightly better than his foe, but if your starting pitcher is slightly better than *his* foe, you do not have a tie. The team with the pitcher is far ahead.

Yet even in pitching, there were some who thought the Yankees had the edge. After all, Whitey Ford would start for New York. Ford was five-and-one in World Series opening games. How much more head-to-head can you get? After Ford there were such blazing youngsters as Al Downing and Jim Bouton, and a man as good as Ralph Terry would sit in the bullpen in this Series. That's how good the Yankee pitching was. What did the Dodgers have to pit against such a lineup?

You could fault this Dodger team at bat, but you do not pay off in batting averages. The Cards and Giants outhit the Dodgers in '63. You pay off in victories. The Dodgers—scoring fewer runs than four other teams in the league—won the pennant. They did it by winning the close ones. The Dodgers won 34 one-run games; they lost 18. For a team with a batting average of .251—a drop of 17 points from 1962—it was also a team that was shut out less often than any club in the league. It has been said, and it has been said truly, that a Dodger rally is a walk, a stolen base, and a

bloop single hit to the wrong field. You pay off on the scoreboard. A run is a run is a run, even when it is walked home.

But—again—the name of the game is pitching. The Yankees had Ford, Downing, and Bouton? This Dodger team was shut out by the opposition eight times. Its pitchers combined for 24 shutouts, most in the majors, most ever by a Dodger staff. They struck out 1,094 men. The combined earned-run average was a fantastic 2.85, best in baseball, and the first time a staff ERA had dipped under three runs since the Cubs of 1945.

It was a miserly staff, and its big four of Koufax, Drysdale, Podres, and the incredible Ron Perranoski, were even more miserly. Their combined ERA was a 2.45 speck.

Perhaps Whitey Ford could carry glittering clippings to the mound himself, but observers recalled that in the '62 Series, Whitey had been battered his last two appearances. He had won more World Series games than any other pitcher, but he had also lost as many games as any other pitcher.

Besides, just how murderous was that Yankee attack? In his last two Series, Mickey Mantle had batted .167 and .120. Giant pitchers had tied him in frustrated knots in '62; the picture this observer takes home is Mantle pounding his bat on the plate in rage after Jack Sanford had again picked up the outside corner with his curve ball.

Roger Maris had hit .105 and .174 in his last two Series.

And Mantle and Maris are the heart of the Yankee attack.

Much of this is hindsight. We know what happened. But the intention here is to find perspective. Bobby Richardson was a great second baseman for 162 games in 1963, and a man who could not be struck out. Just 22 times in 630 times at bat. Once a week.

In the '63 World Series, the unknown Tracewski played brilliantly in the field; his play in the fifth inning of the first game remains the key defensive move of the entire Series. Richardson—the man who struck out once a week—fanned three times that first game.

And the first game set the pattern for the Series.

For four and two-thirds innings, nobody has ever pitched a better World Series game than had Sandy Koufax in the opener at Yankee Stadium. Don Larsen had pitched one as well, and kept pitching it, but nobody has ever been better for those first fourteen outs.

Koufax struck out the side in the first inning. Tony Kubek swung at a big curve. Richardson swung at inside fast balls. Tom Tresh watched as Koufax bent over that big curve.

In the second inning, right after the demoralized Yankees knew just how good Koufax could be, the Dodgers ripped Ford for four big runs, highlighted by John Roseboro's home run, hit high into the air and hugging the foul line.

Now the game was over. Now the story could be Koufax, the rest of the way. Baseball has a way of clearing the decks for individual exploits. You could focus your eyes on the

young man on the mound. It had become a solo performance.

In the bottom of the second, behind his big four-run lead, Koufax faced Mickey Mantle, batting right-handed. Koufax pitched to Mantle the way Sanford had pitched to him a year ago. He picked up the outside corner with a curve that couldn't have been a half-inch above the knees. Mantle was uneasy at the plate. He reminded you of Willie Mays when Mays is facing a fireballing right-hander. Mays then tends to pull away from the pitch. Ballplayers call it "bailing out." Mantle was bailing out on Koufax, even though there wasn't the same problem of a right-hander facing a right-handed pitcher. Mantle is a switch-hitter. Every pitch must come toward him from a distance away; no pitch comes by way of the rear, or blind side. Yet Mantle was bailing out. He pulled back from a 1-and-2 pitch, probably expecting the curve to bend too far inside. Instead, it was the fast ball, fired across the inside corner. Mantle looked foolish as Joe Paparella called it strike three.

Roger Maris swung on a 2-and-2 fast ball. Missed.

Koufax had struck out the first five Yankee batters. Once before in a World Series had this transpired. Mort Cooper struck out the first five Yankees in the first game of the 1942 Series. The Yankees had gone on to win.

They were not to win this game.

The Dodgers added a run in the third, driven home by Bill Skowron, who was to plague his old bosses throughout the 4-game set.

And that is how it went, Los Angeles leading, 5–0, and Koufax pitching as well as a human being can pitch.

Pepitone went down in the third, swinging at a fast ball. In the fourth, Koufax began working his way through the order again, and the results were the same. He again fanned the side. He struck out Kubek and Richardson—swinging—on big curves, and he got Tresh on a called third strike, blazing in a fast ball.

Now the records were up for grabs. Ten years ago to the day—October 2, 1953—Carl Erskine had struck out 14 Yankees, to break old Howard Ehmke's record of 13 against the Chicago Cubs in 1929. Koufax had 9 in four innings.

When Sandy Koufax is pitching well, he falls into a rhythm that is smooth as glass. The ball is thrown effortlessly, the big beautifully muscled body behaving in flowing coordination that rivals the grace of a ballerina.

Going into the fifth, such was his rhythm. Mantle led off. There was a fast ball on the hands; Mantle fouled it back. Then a fast ball poured through the high part of the strike zone. Mantle, bailing out, waved weakly. Another fast ball was fouled off, but this time Mantle had his vicious cut, falling to his knees at the conclusion. A high fast ball forced Mantle away from the plate. It was inside, for ball one. Another fast ball was high. Then Koufax bent in the curve, and Mantle struck out, swinging. Number ten.

But someplace in pitching to Mantle, the easy grace, the smooth rhythm was temporarily lost. Koufax labored, and

in the process of laboring, he began to work more swiftly. Roseboro would return the ball to Koufax, and Sandy would almost immediately go into his motion.

Roger Maris fouled out to Roseboro on a two-and-two count, and not a ball had been hit past the infield. Roseboro himself was nearing a record for put-outs by a catcher. Perhaps because you cannot argue with success, Roseboro did not come out from behind the plate to slow down his pitcher.

Elston Howard broke the spell, ended the perfect game. He hit an outside curve ball to right field for a single. The Yankees had their first base runner.

Joe Pepitone took a curve for a strike, let a low curve go by for ball one, fouled off a fast ball, took a high curve for ball two, and then pumped a ball into the hole between first and second to right field, for a base hit. Howard, the team's slowest runner, held up at second.

Clete Boyer—the only Yankee regular who would not strike out that day—then hit a Koufax pitch through the middle of the diamond, headed for center field.

From his position to the right of second base, Dick Tracewski came flying over. At the last moment, he lunged for the ball, knocking it down with his gloved hand. It was a spectacular play, and a run-saving play. Howard held up at third. The bases were loaded.

Koufax—who later was to growl that he'd been throwing "too many perfect pitches"—went to work on Hector Lopez, batting for Ford. Still pitching quickly, Koufax bul-

leted in a called strike, missed low with another fast ball, jammed Lopez with a third fast ball which the right-handed batter fouled off, and then missed with his first curve. Perhaps Koufax was having trouble with his curve; perhaps he wasted the curve to set up the fast ball. The next pitch was a blazer, and Lopez, swinging, became Koufax's 11th K.

The inning was over, and the shutout intact. Dick Tracewski had supplied the big play.

Any chance for a run at Koufax's personal strikeout high of 18 became remote in the sixth. For the first time, he failed to strike out a batter.

"I lost my rhythm in the middle innings," Koufax would say later.

It was apparent to any observer. There was a stiffness to his movements, as though all those bunched muscles had tightened into a series of knots throughout his back, his shoulders, his upper arms, his thighs.

Koufax says it was "probably because I was pitching too fast." But there may have been outside circumstances that tended to affect Koufax in the middle innings. A few days before the season closed down, Sandy caught cold. He missed a few days of running in the outfield, keeping up his wind. His legs may have become tired in the middle innings at Yankee Stadium.

"I got a little tired around the sixth and seventh," Koufax said later. "I felt a little weak." But not just in the sixth and seventh innings. They were the worst spots. "I just felt a little tired in general early in the game. Then I felt a little

weak in the middle of the game. Then I got some of my strength back, but I was a little weak at the end."

These are the words of a perfectionist. Another man would have taken this performance and set it up in his mind's eye as a shining example of the art of pitching. Koufax found it lacking.

In the sixth inning, Koufax's motion—in the words of observer Roger Angell—had become "stiff and elbowish." Tony Kubek bounced out to Gilliam. Richardson—who had struck out swinging in the first and fourth—now made Koufax work. Sandy missed with three consecutive fast balls, all high. Then his fast ball picked up the strike zone. Another fast ball clipped the outside corner. Richardson had not offered at a single pitch. Koufax fired outside, and Richardson had the Yankees' first base on balls.

Koufax was upset. At himself. He threw four times to Tom Tresh, and the Yankees had their second walk, and the Stadium had come alive. The Dodgers led by five, but this was not the same Koufax. Three hits the inning before; two walks this inning. A couple of base hits now and the tying run would come to the plate. Tracewski's play took on added import. On the Dodger bench, Alston sat quietly, staring at his pitcher. In the bullpen, there was a stir, and then Bob Miller and Ron Perranoski got up and began to throw.

Koufax took a deep breath. He worked carefully to Mickey Mantle, a man who could slice the five-run lead to two runs with one big swish of his yellow bat.

The count went to two and two, Koufax mixing swift stuff with slower curves, and then he blew in the fast ball, and Mantle lifted it harmlessly to Dick Tracewski.

Now it was Maris. Koufax bent in a called strike, missed low and away with a fast ball, and then poured in another fast ball. Maris popped it weakly to Wills. The inning was over, the threat was past. On the bench, Alston spoke quietly to Koufax. The pitcher nodded.

In the seventh, Elston Howard—who had the team's first hit—struck out on a swinging curve. This was number twelve. There were just seven outs left. Pepitone hit a rare Koufax change-up in the air behind the plate, and Roseboro had another put-out. Boyer also hit a slow pitch, and Wills gathered in the soft fly ball. Koufax had retired the side on eight pitches.

In the eighth, the Yankees broke through. Pinch hitter Phil Linz became Sandy's thirteenth strikeout victim, swinging at a fast ball, and the Erskine record was one away, breaking it was two away.

Kubek hit a ground ball to deep short, where Maury Wills made a fine stop, but there was no chance to nip the speeding Yankee. It was the fourth Yankee hit, and here came the meat of the order. How long could such men as Tresh, Mantle, and Maris be contained?

First, Richardson. The man who never struck out. He swung at three fast balls, and the partisan crowd—rooting for the Yankees—roared. Koufax had caught Erskine. With five outs remaining, it seemed sure he would break the record.

Koufax concentrated on young Tom Tresh. Tresh had been taking strikes. Koufax threw a fast ball, and Tresh belted it. The ball buried itself deep in the lower deck of the left field stands, well away from the foul line. It was a healthy blast, and the Yankees had burst through. The score was 5–2. The shutout was gone; the strikeout record still had not been broken. More important, the Yankees were still alive.

Koufax threw another fast ball to Mantle, and Mick fouled it off. Then Koufax—still troubled by his "elbowish" motion, all angles and sharp edges—missed four times, and Mantle was on.

Out of the Dodger dugout came Alston, trotting. Perranoski and Drysdale were now up in the bullpen, throwing. Memory flits back to another Koufax moment. The game against Cincinnati, in his freshman year, and Alston trotting out in a late inning when Sandy suddenly went wild. Alston settled the youngster then.

What did he say this time?

"I told Sandy to slow down and take it easy. Not to try to pitch too fine to Maris, even if he hit it out of the park. He had been pitching too fast when he walked those two in the sixth, and we tried to slow him down when he came in after that inning, too."

Slow down. Take it easy. *Don't* reach back for that nonsensical something extra. Find your rhythm instead. The rest will take care of itself. Don't work too hard on picking up a corner. Just get the ball in there. If Maris hits it out, you're still a run ahead. But slow down. Slow down.

Koufax fell back on his fast ball. But thrown easily, not forced. Maris hit the ball straight at second baseman Tracewski. The youngster scooped it easily, and rifled to Bill Skowron. The eighth inning was past.

Now it was the ninth. This would be the lower part of the Yankee order, but what difference does it make when the names begin with Elston Howard and Joe Pepitone?

Howard poked a line drive, but again the ball was aimed at Tracewski. Out number one. Pepitone became the only Yankee to get two hits. He hit a Koufax curve to right field.

But Sandy seemed unruffled. His rhythm had returned. He had stopped laboring. Baseballs were coming out of an effortless windup and delivery, and they were dead on target. Boyer hit under the ball, and lofted it straightaway to Willie Davis in center field. Davis threw his arms out, as though to ward off any onrushing outfielder. Then he made the catch in his flamboyant fashion. It was the first fly ball any Yankee had hit to an outfielder.

Only one out remained. The record still had not been broken. The batter was Harry Bright, hitting for reliever Steve Hamilton. Koufax had struck out the other two pinch hitters. In the stands, Carl Erskine watched Koufax on the mound, his own record on the line.

The count went to two-and-two, Koufax throwing all fast balls. Then Bright swung and topped a little ground ball down the third-base line. Had the ball remained in play, Koufax might have thrown him out. The ball spun foul, and the crowd was visibly relieved.

Later, Harry Bright was to say dryly: "I guess I'm the

only batter in baseball to have 69,000 fans cheering for me to strike out." In his home park, too.

Bright obliged them. Koufax wound slowly and let a fast ball fly. The pitch was a white blur. Bright swung savagely. The ball exploded in Roseboro's expectant mitt. Roseboro rushed out and caught Sandy in a fierce embrace. Walt Alston was on the field, congratulating his pitcher. Then a mob of Dodgers descended on Koufax.

The Dodgers had beaten the Yankees, 5–2, to take a one-game lead.

Sandy Koufax had struck out 15 Yankees. Once again, his name had been entered in the record book. In the Dodger dressing room, the man he displaced, Carl Erskine, shook his hand warmly.

The Yankees do not lose often. When they do lose, they lose well and graciously. There is no search for alibis. Yogi Berra said: "I don't see how he lost five games during the season."

Mantle said: "Everything I read about Koufax is true. He's a damn good pitcher." Then he grinned wryly. "I don't feel so bad about striking out twice against him. When Carl Erskine set the old record of fourteen, remember, I struck out four times."

Not that every Yankee was granting Koufax an automatic second win when they saw him in Los Angeles a few days hence. "He's a great pitcher," Tom Tresh said, "as good as anybody in our league. But now that we've had a chance to get a look at him, we'll get to him easier next

time. And you won't see anything like fifteen strikeouts."

Yet Koufax had shaken the Yankees. "He's a lot like Camilo Pascual," Tony Kubek remarked. "Who knows if we'll hit him hard next time? I hope so. But the guys in the National League get to see him all season. Do they hit him any better in September?"

Koufax had won 5 games in September, without a loss.

And when Ralph Houk, Yankee manager, his cap askew, grinning in defeat, was asked to explain the loss, he used one word:

"Koufax."

But nothing is easy, even in an unprecedented 4-game sweep over the noble Yankees.

Unknown to the public, Koufax was entering another arena of pain and discomfort. A corn situated between the last two toes of Sandy's left foot prematurely tore loose before the fourth game of the Series. It left an ugly wound. Dr. Robert Kerlan, Dodger physician, treated the raw, bloodied, ulcerated area.

"It was so tender," Dr. Kerlan explained after the Series had become history, "that you couldn't even apply this much pressure to it." He barely brushed his wrist.

Sandy Koufax had run the gamut of injuries.

From tip to toe.

Back at the Stadium, in the second game, Johnny Podres —the man who had beaten the Yankees twice in the '55 Series, and whom the Yankees had turned down as part of a

trade with the Dodgers—whipped them again, and cut Koufax's two runs in half. Podres weakened in the ninth, and Ron Perranoski pitched the last two outs. The teams flew across the country, and in Los Angeles, Don Drysdale kept up the incredible pitching, and again improved on his predecessors. Drysdale shut out the Yankees, in a game Sandy Koufax later called the "best-pitched game of the Series and of the season."

There was nothing Koufax could do to better Drysdale's performance, except, perhaps, striking out sixteen men, or pitching a perfect no-hitter.

He did neither.

He did enough.

The ulcerated area between the toes was a matter of concern, both to Koufax and Dr. Kerlan. Before the Sunday ball game, Kerlan deadened the region with a local anesthetic. Then the physician set up a series of simple hand signals with the Dodger trainer, sitting on the bench. If the trainer waved his towel out of the dugout, it meant the toes were giving Koufax trouble. If he formed an "O" with his thumb and forefinger, it was the universal sign of all's well.

But Dr. Kerlan is—as he must be—a worrier. So he kept making pilgrimages down from his perch in the press box at Dodger Stadium to the dugout every few innings, to make sure Koufax was not suffering unduly.

Once again, it was Koufax versus Ford, but this time 55,912 fans saw the real Ford, not some ersatz model.

For three innings, Koufax was again his masterful, per-

fect self. Nine Yankees came up and went down, four of them—Kubek, Tresh, Pepitone, and Boyer—on strikes.

Ford was even better. His perfect string went four innings.

In the fourth, Bobby Richardson lofted a fly ball into short center field, where Willie Davis lost it in the sun, and the Yankees had a gift two-base hit. The significance of a ball lost in the dazzling Los Angeles sunlight would not be known for several innings. Koufax settled to his job, and retired Tresh and Mantle.

In the fifth inning, Ford faced big Frank Howard.

Howard is very likely the longest hitter in the entire history of baseball. True enough, he has lively balls and livelier bats on his side, but so do 400 other major-leaguers. Howard outhits them all for distance. When he hits.

In the Series opener, Howard had been served up a pitch he rarely sees anymore. Whitey Ford threw him a fast ball, chest high, over the center of the plate. It was a contemptuous pitch, and if the Yankees have a personality defect, it lies in their almost natural feeling of superiority, a feeling that comes dangerously close to arrogance. Nobody would dare throw a down-the-pipe fast ball to Howard, unless you had no other pitch to throw. Nobody but a Yankee pitcher whose bread-and-butter pitch is a curve ball.

Howard hit the Ford fast ball on a line, as far and as hard as anybody had ever hit a line drive within the playing confines of Yankee Stadium. The ball flew to the most remote

spot in the park, striking the center field fence on the fly, some 460 feet from the plate.

Ford learned his lesson. The book had said Howard had gobs of trouble with outside curve balls. He would often fish for them, finishing his futile swing with one hand on the bat.

So in the fifth inning of the fourth Series game, the score 0–0, and Ford thus far pitching perfectly, Whitey threw a curve in the prescribed manner to big Howard. Sure enough, Frank swung with one hand.

Except he connected.

The ball soared long and deep into the upper deck of the left field seats at Dodger Stadium. Nobody had ever hit a ball into the upper tier before.

The Dodgers led, 1–0.

It was not enough.

In the seventh inning, Mickey Mantle—hapless in five prior shots at Koufax in the Series—timed a fast ball perfectly and hit it over the left center field wall, for a home run that would have seemed of heroic distance, except it followed Howard's. Still, it was a long blast, and it marked the first time the Yankees had tied the Dodgers. In each game the Dodgers had scored first and the Yankees never caught up.

Koufax retired the Yankees after Mantle's home run, and in the eighth inning, Jim Gilliam hit a high bounding ball headed for the left field corner and two-base-hit territory. But Clete Boyer leaped high and speared the bouncer. Then he fired accurately to first.

Boyer's throw came out of a sea of vivid sports shirts. This was Los Angeles, on a typically gorgeous sun-spangled day. The shadows had lengthened, but the sun was still a golden ball in the declining west.

The throw struck Joe Pepitone on the inside of his right forearm, and rolled out into foul ground along the right field line. Gilliam never stopped running until he was on third base.

Willie Davis wasted no time. The Dodgers had just two hits— Frank Howard had them both—but they were going to win this World Series contest without another. Davis drove Ford's pitch a long distance into center field. Mantle caught the ball easily, but even more easily Gilliam breezed home after the out.

Koufax had one inning to go. One inning to close down a magnificent year and right all the ills of 1962. No team had suffered a more bitter defeat than had the Dodgers in '62; now they stood a chance to wipe out that bitter taste which still clung.

In the ninth, Bobby Richardson got his second hit. There was nobody out, and each runner represented the tying run. Each new hitter would represent the lead run. Koufax was tired. It had been a long year, though a great one. The hitters were Tresh and Mantle.

Sandy Koufax got two strikes on Tresh—Tresh, who had hit a home run in the first game, and who had said the Yankees would get to Koufax easier this time. Koufax started a pitch up high, inches outside. Tresh watched the

ball. It veered suddenly—Koufax's big curve ball—and it slashed downward. Without a word, Tresh walked away.

Now it was Mantle, Mantle who had hit a home run his last trip to the plate, Mantle who could crush baseballs with his bat. Again Koufax got in two swift strikes. He readied himself for the next pitch. So did Mantle. So did we.

Koufax came out of his stretch, throwing hard. It began high and outside, to the right-handed hitter, very much like Koufax's fast ball. Mantle relaxed—as Tresh had relaxed—and he took all the way.

And like an eerie echo, or a set of ditto marks, the ball broke jaggedly once more, down and in, and again the umpire thrust up his right hand.

Silently, shaking his head, Mickey Mantle walked away. Later, Mantle dissected the pitch:

"That was some pitch. His curve and his fast ball start out the same way, way up here. You have to set yourself for the fast ball against him or you have no chance at all. Halfway to the plate, you still don't know if it's a fast ball or a curve. If it's a fast ball it looks like it's going to be much too high, so you don't swing. But then it turns out to be a curve and it breaks down out of nowhere right over the plate. And by then it's too late to swing. It was a tremendous pitch. And he's a tremendous pitcher."

It was Koufax's eighth strikeout. Again he had broken a World Series mark, with his total of 23 strikeouts. In 1945, Detroit's Hal Newhouser had struck out 22 Cubs, but it had

taken Newhouser three shots and twenty and two-thirds innings to do the job. Koufax had his 23 in eighteen innings.

Still, the game was not over, and the tying run still stood on first base.

Koufax was a weary young man. "I don't know if I could even have pitched a third game, much less won it," he said later. "I was that tired."

Elston Howard stepped in. Howard hit a ball to the bare-hand side of Maury Wills. Wills slid over, made the grab, and fired to second where Bobby Richardson was going into his slide. The throw was slightly low. Dick Tracewski reached, and appeared to make the catch. The umpire's hand flew up—for the out signal—and on the mound, turned to watch the action, Sandy Koufax gave a little involuntary leap of joy. Then the ball trickled away from Tracewski, and the umpire's arm hastily slashed down to change his call. This time you could see the jolting emotion of dismay cross Koufax's face.

Recuperating from his heart seizure at home, Irving Koufax could not stand to watch his son, could not stand to watch the tense situation that enveloped the mound. He turned off his television set. "I felt a little flutter," he said. Sandy described his own emotions to writer Milton Gross. "I felt a little flutter, too. It was almost too much for me."

Almost. But not quite. He had a job to do. Now the tying run was on second. A base hit would undoubtedly score Richardson. Howard, on first, represented the go-ahead run. Koufax was pitching his 329th inning of the year. The hitter

was Hector Lopez, a dangerous right-handed hitter, slow of foot. Keep the ball down. Make him hit it to the infield.

Lopez swung at a low fast ball, hit it on the ground. Wills rushed in. "Throw it, Maury!" Koufax shouted. "Throw it!"

Maury threw it.

Sandy Koufax was $12,794 richer.

The bitterness of 1962 was totally dissolved.

The mighty Yankees had been humbled in a way unknown to them.

In the press box, Al Silverman of *Sport* magazine announced to the reporters: "Koufax wins the Corvette. Koufax wins the Corvette."

On the field, ecstatic Dodgers threw themselves all over Koufax.

In the clubhouse, twenty-four-year-old Tommy Davis came over to Koufax's cubicle and said: "Sandy, you are the greatest pitcher that ever lived." Davis had never seen Johnson, Mathewson, Waddell, Alexander, Grove or Hubbell. He had never seen Feller. But maybe—just maybe—he was right.

And in the Dodger dressing room, Koufax set himself behind a table, and as the reporters surged forward to get their stories, Sandy said with a mischievous grin at his lips:

"Gentlemen, you probably are wondering why I've called this little conference."

12

"I'll Be as Straight as I Can Be."

WHO IS SANDY KOUFAX?

He is a liberal tipper, as most athletes are.

He drinks and smokes in extremely small quantities. He refuses to sit still for cigarette- or liquor-advertising testimonials. He does not like to be photographed, either smoking or drinking.

He does not talk about his dates.

He owns three or four suits, eight to ten sports jackets, eight to ten pairs of slacks, a half-dozen or so vivid alpaca sweaters.

He owns a piece of the Tropicana Motel, on Sunset Boulevard in Los Angeles. He owns a piece of an FM stereo station in Thousand Oaks, California, out in the San Fernando Valley. When he pitched his no-hitter against the Giants, Sandy turned down offers to go to parties that night. Instead, he had promised to go to the FM station and participate in an all-night fund-raising charity show. He went.

He lives in a ten-year-old contemporary house in Studio City, California. He loves to putter about the house, except in the garden. He hates gardening. He stocks his house with good books, paintings, and some 200 phonograph records,

only a small part of which is longhair, despite all you hear to the contrary.

His vice is music. When he wakes at home, he turns on his radio, his stereo set, or his tape. On the road he carries, in an oversized attaché case, a portable radio and a tape recorder. Sometimes Leo Durocher snarls good-naturedly: "Give it a rest, why don'tcha, Sandy?" Sandy seldom gives it a rest.

He does not know what he'll do when his career ends, but he thinks he may go back to college.

He considers himself shy. It embarrasses him when he has to make a speech or sit on a dais, as he had to do thirty to forty times after the 1963 season ended.

He says his first impulse when a horde of fans converges on him is to flee. He does not like being on display.

"Whatever I do off the field," he says, "outside of baseball, after baseball, is my own business, so long as I don't cause trouble. If I live alone, well, so what? If I like to do something, who has to know? Who cares? I'm no different than anyone else. I figure my life is my own to live as I want. Is that asking too much?"

He says he is not a loner, but to a certain degree, he surely is. "I like to go to sleep when I feel like it," he says, "get up at what hour suits me, listen to the music I prefer, and watch what I enjoy on TV. It's not, however, that I like being alone. If I lived in a hotel room, I'd probably never stay in the room." Yet in hotel rooms, on the road, he cuts off the phone and tries to sleep until noon.

He does not enjoy being interviewed. A sportswriter paid him this rare tribute:

"He is one of the few ball players—Don Drysdale is another—whom you can talk to when things are bad for them. Even when he's taken a beating, he grits his teeth and holds his head up, and answers your questions."

He never alibis.

He says the best thing about baseball is "now I'm excited about playing."

But he admits the excitement cannot remain at a high peak all season. "By the time the season's nearly over, my interest has waned."

What he does not enjoy, is baseball's "80-hour week." He finds road trips—travel—"the roughest of all. You hit a town, check into a hotel, go to the ball park, come back to the hotel, sleep a while. It's hard to tell Cincinnati from Pittsburgh. I know San Francisco because it's so cold. My arm feels the worst there. And I know Houston because it's so hot."

He thinks Henry Aaron is the game's best hitter. "You can't fool him. He has quick reflexes and is ready for anything you throw."

He never lets his personal achievements interfere with the purpose of the game—to win. Once he was congratulated for posting strikeout number 1,000.

"So what?" Sandy snapped. "I lost, didn't I?"

He still must answer questions about his finger. The finger does not bother him. But he knows it is there. "At times I can feel a hard spot inside the finger, which is scar tissue.

When the callus on the skin becomes too large and tender, I rub it with pumice."

He does not deliberately set pitching goals for himself, although he has some long-range ambitions. "I'm not trying to set records for shutouts, no-hitters, or anything of the sort," he says. "I take baseball one inning at a time, one game at a time. If I've done well at the end of a season, then I can think about bigger goals."

His bigger goals are to win over 350 games in his career. Only Spahn—among modern pitchers, and among National League left-handers—has won 350 times.

Koufax says he keeps a mental card file on every hitter in the league. But he adds ruefully that he supposes it does him no good. Every batter in the league—he points out—keeps a mental card file on him.

He does not pretend that he has solved all the problems, either those of pitching or those of maturing. Sometimes he forgets the intricacies and subtleties of his craft, and rears back and just chucks the ball. "You have to have an idea," he explains, "some sort of play on every pitch, but sometimes you get tired and forget. Pitchers talk to each other, you know, and one of the things we're agreed on is that when a pitcher gets tired, generally the first thing that gets tired is his head. Then he becomes a thrower instead of a pitcher."

He says he makes mistakes. "Maybe the worst is getting mad at myself when I walk anybody, or make a bad pitch. People say I look poker-faced and don't show emotion. But sometimes things bubble up inside of me and burst out."

But whatever the mistakes, he is really an accomplished craftsman. "He never beats himself," Walt Alston says. "You don't get many cheap runs off him. Anything you get, you work for."

He may allow that the batters have a book on him, but he exudes confidence on the mound. Larry Sherry says of Sandy Koufax: "He knows—he just plain *knows* he's going to get them out."

He is loyal to the organization. Writer Bill Libby tells how Buzzie Bavasi telephoned Sandy after the second no-hitter and offered Koufax a financial reward.

"You don't owe me a thing," Koufax said quickly. "You've been too good to me already." Los Angeles had given Sandy a generous raise, after he had sat out nearly half of 1962. "I'll never forget."

Sandy Koufax is a grateful man. You can pile up on one side of the ledger the sprained ankles, the nightmare finger of 1962, the sore arms and shoulders, the rib tumor, the ulcerated toes. You can add to that the discouragement of the first several years, his own wildness, the club's ignoring of him. You can put on top of all that the monotony of a ballplayer's life, the intrusion of fans and writers, the demands on his time which slowly but surely eat small pieces out of his life.

And he is grateful. "It's been a good life, baseball," he says. "I owe it a lot. I intend to pay it back. I'll be as good a pitcher as I can be. I'll be as straight as I can be."

And is there a biggest thrill, so far?

There have been many big thrills. The two 18-strikeout performances. The two no-hitters. The two wins over the Yankees in the 1963 World Series. The 15 strikeouts in that first 1963 Series game. His first major-league win. Which of these makes for Sandy Koufax's biggest thrill?

None.

His biggest thrill—says Sandy Koufax—came about after his second World Series win, but it was not the win itself, nor the realization that the mighty Yankees had been trampled four straight. The biggest thrill was a more subtle thing, to Sandy Koufax. A news photo helped Sandy Koufax express what that thrill actually was. The picture showed a mob of Dodgers descending on Koufax, to congratulate him after the second win. The caption beneath the photo read: *Teammates go wild for Sandy Koufax who wrapped it all up in four.*

That was his biggest thrill, Sandy Koufax said, tapping the caption.

Coming through for his teammates.

The Author

ARNOLD HANO was voted Magazine Sportswriter of the Year (1963) by editors of 22 magazines, capping a ten-year career as full-time writer. Before that, he was a newspaper reporter, book editor, and high school English teacher. He is the author of several hundred magazine features and three sports books.

Mr. Hano lives in Laguna Beach, California, a location handy to the home park of the Los Angeles Dodgers.

D0561468